Queensland Art Gallery

RETROSPECT AND PROSPECT

The Fine Arts Press· Sydney 1983

Contents

Edited by Mervyn Horton

Copyright © is retained by the authors.

This book is sold subject to the condition that it shall not, by way of trade, be lent, re-sold, hired out or otherwise circulated without the publisher's prior consent, in any form of binding or cover other than that in which it is published and without a similar condition being imposed on the subsequent purchaser. All rights reserved. No part of this publication may be reproduced or transmitted, in any form or by any means, without permission. First published in 1983 by Sam Ure Smith at The Fine Arts Press, Sydney.

This book contains a reprint of pages 477-536 of *ART and Australia*, and has been reprinted by kind permission of the proprietors, The Fine Arts Press Pty Ltd.

ISBN 86917 009 0
Designed by Janet Gough
Typeset by Walter Deblaere & Associates
Printed in Japan by Dai Nippon

Queensland Art Gallery:
A personal view *by Raoul Mellish*

This special number of *ART and Australia* marks the first anniversary of the opening of the new Queensland Art Gallery in June 1982. Nearly 400,000 people visited the new Gallery in the first six months of operation and the Gallery hosted eighteen temporary exhibitions from international and Australian sources.

It is particularly fitting that the Gallery and its Collection should be surveyed at this significant time in the Gallery's history.

Traditionally, major art galleries throughout the world have been distinctive edifices of architectural merit, housing significant collections and promoting high standards in the visual arts. The new Queensland Art Gallery continues in this tradition. In this fine building, designed by Robin Gibson and Partners and winner of the 1982 Sir Zelman Cowen Award for architectural excellence, both the State's own Collection and a wide range of international and other special exhibitions can be presented to great effect.

The earliest move to establish a State art gallery in Queensland was made in 1883, but it was not until 1895 that the Queensland National Art Gallery was opened in a room in the old Town Hall Building — the first of a series of temporary and inadequate premises. Over the years, requests were made to successive Governments for a new Gallery building and, in 1969, as a result of a submission by the Trustees, the State Government set up a

special committee to choose a site for the building. Although it was originally intended that the Gallery alone would occupy the site chosen on the South Bank of the Brisbane River, the project was later enlarged to include buildings for the Queensland Museum, State Library, and a major Performing Arts Centre in the one complex — to be known as the Queensland Cultural Centre.

As Director of the Queensland Art Gallery since 1974 and Assistant Director from 1968, it has been my privilege to be involved in the full development of the Gallery, from temporary premises with a handful of staff and poor facilities, to an institution of international standing with superb facilities and a large professional staff. The last fourteen years have been the most dramatic in the Gallery's history.

As well as the construction of the Gallery building, there have been important new developments in the last few years in the Gallery's Collection.

In 1979, the Queensland Art Gallery Foundation was established to enlist community financial support for major purchases. With the Major Harold de Vahl Rubin gift, in 1959, of seven French works by Picasso, Degas, Vlaminck, Toulouse-Lautrec and Renoir, the Gallery acquired the nucleus of a significant European Collection. The first work purchased by the Queensland Art Gallery Foundation, in 1980, with funds donated by the Utah Foundation, was a late fifteenth-century Netherlandish panel painting by the Master of Frankfurt, *Virgin and Child with Saint James the Pilgrim, Saint Catherine and the Donor with Saint Peter, c.* 1496. Tintoretto's *The Resurrection* of the 1550s, an outstanding Genoese portrait by van Dyck, *Portrait of the Marchese Filippo Spinola, c.* 1622-27, and Sir Peter Paul Rubens's *Portrait of a young woman in a fur wrap* (after Titian), *c.* 1629-39, were all purchased with Foundation funding in 1980. Money donated to the Foundation by M.I.M. Holdings Limited allowed the Gallery to augment its European sculpture collection with the exquisite bronze *Hercules and Omphale* by Foggini, *c.* 1700.

Since its initial emphasis on European works, the acquisitions programme of the Foundation has expanded to include important works by Australian and non-European artists. Most recently, in 1982, the Gallery purchased through the Foundation a major work by Fred Williams, *Echuca landscape,* 1961. The Gallery, since its earliest years, has emphasized the acquisition of works by Australian artists, and Australian art is still the strongest area of the Collection, as this publication shows.

In the future, the Gallery hopes to increase holdings of Asian, modern American, African and Oceanic art.

The facilities of the new Gallery have allowed it to develop new exhibitions initiatives. The Gallery's 'A Survey of Contemporary Australian Crafts exhibition, 1982, and the exhibition 'L.J. Harvey and His School,' 1983, are the important beginnings in a series of Australian exhibitions initiated and curated by the Gallery.

The new Queensland Art Gallery, with its feeling of space and light, challenges the imagination of the Curator, the Exhibitions Designer and the public who come to see the exhibitions. Great emphasis is placed on the temporary exhibitions programme and the design and planning of exhibition spaces. We see the building as a flexible whole in which temporary exhibitions are integrated with the permanent Collection in varying locations.

The official opening of the new Queensland Art Gallery on 21 June 1982 was marked by five international Exhibitions: 'Japan: Masterpieces from the Idemitsu Collection' from Tokyo; 'Kandinsky' from the Guggenheim Museum, New York; 'The World of Edward Hopper ' from the Whitney Museum of American Art, New York; 'Town, Country, Shore and Sea: British Drawings and Watercolours from van Dyck to Nash ' from the Fitzwilliam Museum, Cambridge, and 'Renaissance Bronzes from the Victoria and Albert Museum and Renaissance Bronzes and Related Drawings from the Ashmolean Museum, Oxford'. Following this, for the 1982 Commonwealth Games, the Gallery presented a further eight exhibitions from within Australia and throughout the Commonwealth.

The Queensland Art Gallery has been mindful of its Statewide commitment. A major focus of planning is the Extension Services Programme. In December 1982, the Gallery sent the international exhibition, 'Fabric and Form: New Textile Art from Britain', to the Perc Tucker Regional Gallery in Townsville. At the same time, four educational exhibitions toured to north Queensland. Future Extension Services will include education programmes as well as curatorial and conservation advice to regional galleries.

The Education Programme has been designed to form an integral part of the new Gallery's overall programme. In my overseas trips, in 1973 as a Churchill Fellow and, again, in 1975, I made special note of education programmes in the United States. In 1981, the Gallery was one of three museums chosen, world-wide, to take part in an international exchange with American museums of senior museum education staff, which allowed the then Senior Education Officer (now Assistant Director), Mrs Caroline Launitz-Schurer, to observe the very latest trends in education programmes. The aim of our Education Programme is to make the Gallery and its Collection and exhibitions accessible and comprehensible to all visitors. The Education Section in the new Gallery has a lecture theatre and working studio for art classes, and, importantly, an artist-in-residence studio. The Gallery also has first-class conservation facilities and a public reading-room attached to the reference library.

The Queensland Art Gallery is now ready to fulfil its challenging role of providing for the needs of the people of Queensland in all aspects of the visual arts.

Queensland Art Gallery:
An historical perspective

by Janet Hogan

DAPHNE MAYO   PORTRAIT OF R. GODFREY RIVERS
c. 1925-27
Bronze   39 × 30 × 25 cm
Gift of Mrs Selina Rivers, 1929

This bust of the man who was instrumental in the initial opening of the Gallery in 1895, 'rightly occupied a place of honour near the entrance' when the Gallery reopened in 1931 in its third premises.

Janet Hogan is Research and Publications Officer at the Queensland Art Gallery. She is an experienced writer and lecturer on the arts in Australia.

Photographs of works in the Queensland Art Gallery Collection are by Richard Stringer and Ray Fulton.

When the new Queensland Art Gallery opened on the South Bank of the Brisbane River in June 1982, it seemed that the hopes expressed at the Gallery's initial opening in 1895 were at last being realized — that the beginning of the Gallery, though 'small and humble . . . would be the beginning of a very fine one'.

The Queensland Government acquired several art works by gift in the 1880s and early 1890s, conditional upon their forming part of a national gallery when established. Such acquisitions included a group of seventeenth-century Dutch paintings 'of considerable value', bequeathed by Queensland pastoralist and politician, Thomas Lodge Murray-Prior, in 1892.

Concurrently, public interest in art was increasing in Brisbane and various proposals for an art gallery were presented to the Government. In 1887, the Queensland Art Society was formed through the activities of the artists Isaac Walter Jenner, Oscar Fristrom and L.W.K. Wirth, and in 1895 a Gallery ultimately opened through the efforts of artist Godfrey Rivers, who arrived from England in 1889 and subsequently became Art Master at the Technical College and President of the Art Society.

A supplement to the *Queensland Government Gazette* on Monday, 25 March 1895 announced that 'His Excellency the Governor, with the advice of the Executive Council, has been pleased to establish a Public Art Gallery in Brisbane, to be called "The Queensland National Art Gallery" . . .' On the following Friday the Gallery was opened to the public by the Governor, Sir Henry Norman, 'in presence of a large gathering of ladies and gentlemen'. The opening exhibition was hung by Godfrey Rivers and included his *Woolshed, New South Wales*, a gift to the Gallery, and many works lent for the occasion.

The first premises of the Gallery comprised a large upper room of Brisbane's then Town Hall, 'placed at the disposal of the Trustees by the Municipal Council'. The collection initially under the control of the Trustees consisted of 'thirty-eight pictures (many of which had been lent to the Gallery), one marble bust, and seventy engravings'. The first President of Trustees was the Chief Justice of Queensland, Sir Samuel Walker Griffith, and Godfrey Rivers acted as Secretary to the Trustees from their appointment. Rivers was also the first Curator, from 1898-1914/15.

Early gifts to the new Gallery included Jenner's *Cape Chudleigh, Coast of Labrador* and Fristrom's *Duramboi*, donated by the artists. The Gallery's first purchase was a British work, Blandford Fletcher's *Evicted*, in 1896, and its first Australian purchase was Josephine Muntz-Adams's *Care*, in 1898. In 1899 the initial Government grant of £500 had risen to £1,000 and, by 1900, the Trustees had decided to appoint a committee in

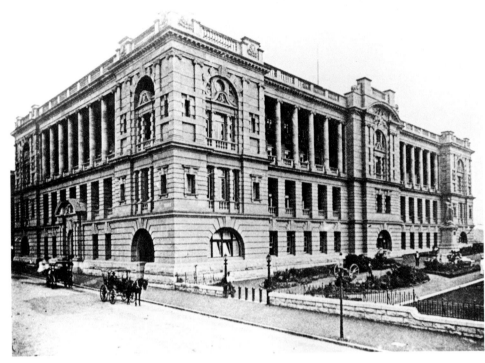

left
On 18 December 1905, the Gallery reopened in the recently completed Executive Building (now Land Administration Building), where it remained until 1930.
Reproduced courtesy the John Oxley Library, Brisbane

below
The Gallery opened in 1895 in the now demolished Town Hall building, in a large upper room placed at the disposal of the Trustees by the Municipal Council.
Reproduced courtesy the John Oxley Library, Brisbane

London to assist with the selection of works of art in Europe. However, by 1904-05 the annual grant had dropped to £100, which was insufficient to meet expenses, including the rent of £50.

At the same time, more adequate accommodation was being considered. In his speech at the opening of the Gallery in 1895, the Governor said he 'hoped that it would not be long before it would be necessary to provide a more suitable building for the Gallery'. By July 1896, the Trustees reported that 'the present location of the Gallery is . . . inconvenient, and we are strongly of opinion that its interest and usefulness would be much increased if a more easily accessible site were available'. These sentiments were repeated annually until the Gallery was relocated at the newly constructed Executive Building in George Street (present Land Administration Building) and reopened on 18 December 1905.

In 1906, 1907 and 1909 travelling exhibitions were organized by the Gallery to enable the people in remote areas of Queensland to view its Collection; but, subsequently, as artist Vida Lahey said, 'somnolence reigned'

for approximately twenty years.

During 1929-30 the former Exhibition Building Concert Hall, erected in 1891, was remodelled to house the Gallery which moved there in 1930, providing further room for its Collection. The Gallery reopened to the public on 11 February 1931 and was officially opened by the Governor, Sir John Goodwin, on 8 April. A bust of Godfrey Rivers, sculpted by Daphne Mayo, 'rightly occupied a place of honour near the entrance'. Nearby was Rivers's *Woolshed, New South Wales,* and Vida Lahey's *Monday morning.*

Lahey and Mayo were prime movers in the establishment of the Queensland Art Fund, launched in April 1929 'to awaken interest by showing works of art to the people' and 'to purchase overseas art works'. At the Gallery opening in 1931, the Fund presented the first of many acquisitions with which it enriched the Gallery's Collection for several years. The Fund also ensured fulfilment of the financial terms of the John Darnell Bequest in the early 1930s, thereby securing this important bequest for the Gallery.

An endowment from Mrs Selina Rivers in 1932, in memory of her husband, established

G.H.M. ADDISON   UNTITLED   (Architect's drawing of the Exhibition Building, Gregory Terrace)   c. 1890
Ink and gouache on light-brown, heavy, smooth paper
17 × 110cm
Gift of H.S. McDonald Esq., 1958

The Exhibition Building's Concert Hall provided the Gallery's premises from 1930 to 1974.

the Godfrey Rivers Trust for the purchase of works for the Collection, the highlight to date being William Dobell's *The Cypriot*. This was only the beginning of several gifts and bequests made to the Gallery, such as the Rubin Gift in 1959, enabling the purchase of an important group of French works, including the Gallery's most valuable painting, Picasso's *La belle hollandaise*, and, more recently, the many works gifted from the collection of Sir Leon and Lady Trout.

In recognition of the importance of encouraging children in art, the Trustees instituted the Children's Creative Art Classes in 1941. Initially organized by Vida Lahey, they are still held at the Gallery on Saturday mornings.

It was 1949 before the first Director — Robert Campbell — was appointed to the Gallery and, from this time, the Gallery has continued to strengthen. Campbell was succeeded by Robert Haines (1951-60), Laurie Thomas (1961-67), James Wieneke (1967-74), and Raoul Mellish, the present Director, appointed in 1974. Each has made his own particular contribution to the Gallery's development.

In 1951, to celebrate the Commonwealth Jubilee, a specially selected Australian exhibition from the Gallery's Collection toured Queensland in the 'Jubilee Art Train', bringing art to people in country areas. This was followed in 1962 by an 'Aerial Art Exhibition'.

Jubilee Year also witnessed the foundation of the National Gallery Society of Queensland, renamed the Queensland Art Gallery Society in 1960, to stimulate public interest in and raise funds for the Gallery.

The Half Dozen Group of artists, established in Brisbane in 1941 under the guidance of Mrs Lilian Pedersen, presented £500 to the Gallery in 1951 to provide funds for a biennial drawing prize in memory of prominent local craftsman and teacher, L. J. Harvey. Also in the same year, the Trustees instituted what is now known as the Trustees Purchase Exhibition, one of the richest of its kind in Australia. Subsequently, a generous endowment from Lilian Pedersen in 1975 established the Andrew and Lilian Pedersen Memorial Prizes Fund — for drawing, printmaking, and small sculpture competitions.

Agitation continued throughout the

VIDA LAHEY MONDAY MORNING 1912
Oil on canvas 153 × 122 cm
Gift of Mme Emily Coungeau, through the Queensland Art Society, 1912

This painting was located close to Mayo's bust of Rivers at the 1931 opening. Both women were prominent in the formation of the Queensland Art Fund which presented several acquisitions to the Gallery at the 1931 opening and subsequently.

top
IVOR HELE   ROBERT CAMPBELL ESQ.
1955
Oil on composition board   91 × 76 cm
Purchased 1956

Campbell was appointed the first Director of the Gallery in 1949.

right
JOSEPHINE MUNTZ-ADAMS   CARE   1897
Oil on composition board   83 × 69 cm
Purchased 1898

This was the first Australian work purchased by the Gallery.

above
A view from Queen Street c. 1875, looking across the first
Victoria Bridge to the site of the present Queensland Art Gallery.
Reproduced courtesy the John Oxley Library, Brisbane

opposite
Overlooking the Brisbane River at South Brisbane, the Gallery's
first permanent premises were opened on 21 June 1982.

Photographs by Richard Stringer

years for fine, adequate, permanent premises befitting the State's Art Gallery and proposals were made for various sites — without success. However, on 23 December 1968 the Trustees presented a submission to the Government on the inadequacies of the Gallery's facilities and on this occasion positive action resulted. The present site overlooking the Brisbane River at South Brisbane was approved for purchase in April 1969 and a Steering Committee was appointed to establish general guidelines for design and planning for the new building. After a limited two-stage competition, architects Robin Gibson and Partners were announced the winners, on 16 April 1973.

Subsequently, the concept was expanded into the Queensland Cultural Centre, with the Art Gallery as Stage 1 of a complex to include a Performing Arts Centre, the Queensland Museum and the State Library. On 26 June 1975, Robin Gibson and Partners were appointed to prepare an integrated design concept for the Centre, which was approved in October 1975. As the completed first stage, the Queensland Art Gallery now contributes significantly to the architectural and cultural heritage of Australia.

Meanwhile, the Gallery had moved yet again to its fourth temporary premises, in the M.I.M. Building in Ann Street, where it reopened on 25 March 1975. Subsequent to the flood rains and gale-force winds of January 1974, the Gallery had been forced to close to the public from 5 April and move from the former Exhibition Building. It was whilst the Gallery was in the M.I.M. Building that the Queensland Art Gallery Foundation was established in 1979 'in recognition of the need for community support in the Government's efforts in advancing our State's cultural development'.

The Gallery remained in the M.I.M. Building until 1982. At the historic official opening of the new premises on 21 June 1982 the Minister for Tourism, National Parks, Sport and the Arts, the Honourable J. A. Elliott, said that he hoped the new Gallery would be 'a dynamic, ever-changing place that Queenslanders in the next century will come to for stimulation, spiritual replenishment and intellectual reward'. That evening, an estimated 8,000 visitors paid overwhelming tribute to the Gallery when it opened to the public in its first permanent home — after eighty-seven years.

Interior architecture of the Queensland Art Gallery

by Peter Prystupa

The great isolated lonely man may be a great painter or great composer but only the great man who loves people can be a great architect.
Mario G. Salvadori

The primary and most important element in the hands of a creative architect is space.

The quality of space depends on the skilful use of various secondary elements, such as proportions, texture of building materials, light and shade, colour and above all, imagination. We are constantly exposed to spaces created by man and we can be influenced by them in many various ways.

Art gallery experts and visitors to art galleries alike expect the art gallery building — housing and displaying great works of art — to be, in itself, a work of art. Nevertheless, the fact that many important galleries throughout the world are works of art in their own right does not guarantee that they are good art galleries. Gallery buildings are too often monumental concrete sculptures externally, with cathedral-like spaces inside, where space and acrobatics of structural elements dominate and confuse the unfortunate visitor, who stands there in silent trepidation — cut to size.

The potential of the art gallery building for displaying works of art within, and consideration for works of art and visitors generally, are basic and most important qualities. They have been realized in a perfect and harmonious balance in Robin Gibson's new art gallery building in Brisbane. Gibson's long association with visual arts, his love for people, his capacity for work, always seeking perfection, his enthusiasm for architecture, combined with an informed and understanding client, produced outstanding results.

Gibson loves Brisbane, its people, and the river which played such an important part in the growth of the city. Until now the potentials of the Brisbane River have not been fully recognized; in fact, the river was mistreated and abused by industry, traffic engineers and planning authorities. The sensitive siting of the Queensland Cultural Centre, including the art gallery building, on its banks makes use of the river's enhancing and complementary quality. As the first major building on the south side of the Brisbane River, the Gallery established a standard of scale and quality for future architectural development.

Peter Prystupa, Dip. Ing. (Vienna), L.F.R.A.I.A., is Honorary Curator of Architecture and Design at the Queensland Art Gallery. He has been involved in the design of major Government buildings in Queensland.

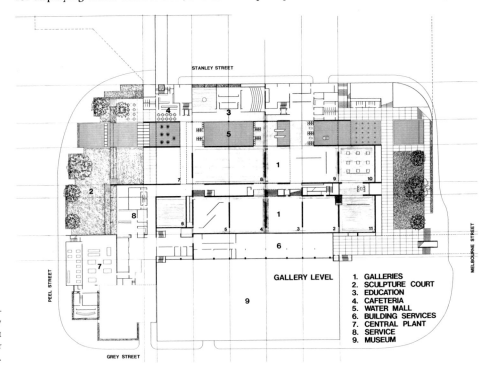

GALLERY LEVEL

1. GALLERIES
2. SCULPTURE COURT
3. EDUCATION
4. CAFETERIA
5. WATER MALL
6. BUILDING SERVICES
7. CENTRAL PLANT
8. SERVICE
9. MUSEUM

top
Gallery 4, temporary exhibitions, adjoining Water Mall area.

Photograph by Richard Stringer

above
INTERNATIONAL DIRECTIONS IN GLASS ART
Exhibition in Gallery 9.

Photograph by Ray Fulton

right
View towards Sculpture Gallery, centre, and walkways above.

Photograph by Richard Stringer

The outline of the complex complements the magnificent silhouettes of the distant mountain ranges. Its effect of light and shade underlines the Mediterranean-like quality of Brisbane's climate.

Covered walkways to three external sides of the Gallery, open to people at all times, offer to passers-by an opportunity for looking inside. They also provide a physical link with other buildings of the Cultural Centre. Architecturally, they are unmistakably Queensland in character, echoing the familiar verandahs of Queensland houses.

Entering the spacious and flexible entrance foyer, the visitor is introduced to the building. The foyer is the point of arrival and departure and is centrally located in relation to the Information Centre, Book Shop, Audio-Visual Theatrette, Library, Education Section with its Studio and Lecture Theatre and the Art Gallery Society area. It extends into Gallery 2. From here one overlooks the central element of the building, the impressive and unique Water Mall space.

Water has been used for thousands of years as an architectural design element. Such use was often based on need, religious ritual or simply on providing pleasure. In China and Japan, water is treasured for the delight it offers to the senses and to the experience it provides, relating man to nature.

Water as a major design element is a new concept in the design of an art gallery anywhere and some technical problems had to be overcome in the Queensland Art Gallery to ensure its correct integration with a desirable environment for works of art.

The Water Mall space extends through three floors, flanked by the horizontality of work floors on one side and a concrete wall on the other. Above, an elegant system of shaped concrete beams diffuses natural light from the skylight.

The mall of water, with its internal and external pools, fountain systems and submerged jets runs parallel to the Brisbane River, along the full extent of the Gallery. It forms a spine to various public and Gallery spaces along and above, and is an excellent orientation element for visitors.

In addition to being a fundamental, functional design concept, the Water Mall both breaks the boundaries between various displays and is an independent work of art in itself. *Bather,* the 218-centimetre high bronze by Emilio Greco, stands in one of the internal water pools and feels absolutely right with the water at its feet. This gives one a foretaste for the exciting possibilities of relating sculpture and water in future displays.

From the entrance foyer, the escalator brings the visitor down to the Water Mall level, where he has a choice of various displays. He may then proceed to Gallery 3, the Sculpture Gallery, visually connected with the external Sculpture Courtyard by a glass wall; a walkway, floating above, invites visitors to view sculptures from a higher vantage point.

Anywhere within the Gallery one is constantly aware of a strong design — discipline and superb detailing. The glazed balustrading to walkways is an example of the elegant simplicity. With the exception of Galleries 4, 7, 9 and 14, which have Tasmanian oak flooring, all galleries are carpeted. Along the walls of all galleries, regardless of flooring, a narrow travertine border strip has been provided, similar to the flooring of all public spaces. The change from wood or carpet to stone is a gentle psychological barrier between viewer and displayed object, providing a clear joint between walls and floors and has a unifying influence on all floors of the Gallery building.

Flexibility of the Temporary Gallery, Gallery 4, with enormous sliding doors at each of the four corners, has been already successfully demonstrated. Despite its huge volume, it provided a superb venue for the intimate masterpieces from the Idemitsu Collection of Japanese art. The almost domestic scale required for the display was achieved by providing an appropriate system of temporary screens and ceiling members and by special lighting.

The voluminous space of Gallery 5, at present displaying large tapestries by Jean Lurçat, which can be overlooked from Gallery 2 above, flows into Gallery 6. Through Gallery 6, the Watercolour Gallery, one reaches Galleries 7, 8 and 9 equipped with display cases for small art objects.

The flexibility of Galleries 10 to 13 is enhanced by suspended movable display screens. An experimental Gallery, Gallery 14, can be closed off from the other display areas if required for visual, sound and other required effects.

Gallery 15, the Corridor Gallery, with its sand-blasted white concrete walls, is ideally suited for display of Graphic Arts and Architecture. It is a continuation of the walkway, which commences at the entrance foyer, leads along the glass wall of the Library, through the upper space of the Water Mall area and the Sculpture Gallery, back to the foyer, linking visually with various other galleries on the way. All public spaces and all work areas have natural light and are visually related to the landscaped outdoors. Of all fifteen gallery spaces, only the Sculpture Gallery has natural light.

The imaginatively placed interlocking public spaces, between groups of galleries, take full advantage of external landscaped areas. One has the feeling that the entire Gallery with its pulsating Water Mall and its plants, is alive. That is, indeed, a rare phenomenon in an art gallery anywhere.

The new Queensland Art Gallery combines the simplicity of whitewashed walls with the sophistication of the contemporary philosophy of architecture and present-day technology.

Queensland's National Gallery: The opening collection, 1895

by Margaret Maynard

THE ODDS AGAINST HER.   Gasking cartoon in the *Queenslander*, 13 April 1895

Margaret Maynard, M.A., completed her studies at the Courtauld Institute, London, and is a lecturer in Fine Arts at the University of Queensland. She has a particular interest in Australian social imagery.

Lagging well behind Victoria, South Australia and New South Wales, Queensland's National Gallery opened more or less permanently to the public for the first time on Friday afternoon, 29 March, 1895.[1] The modesty of this exhibition makes an interesting comparison to the opening of Brisbane's lavish new Cultural Centre on the city's South Bank. Hung not in a costly new building complex but given temporary quarters in the upstairs room of the Town Hall, the Collection consisted of a curious mixture of second-rate Old Masters and contemporary works and included both copies and originals. Culled from the town's meagre artistic resources the incohesive display was largely a reflection of the disparate taste of local art collectors. It was a struggling attempt to place Brisbane a step away from provincialism (an attempt perhaps unrealized even today) and a visible token of her supposed progress toward the cultural refinement already demonstrated by Sydney and Melbourne.

Out of a total of twenty-five oils, thirteen, originally owned by the Colony, formed the core of the Collection. Eleven of these came from a Bequest, finalized in 1894, on behalf of the well-known and status-conscious pastoralist and politician, the Honourable Thomas Lodge Murray-Prior who had died two years before. These were minor sixteenth- and seventeenth-century Italian and Netherlandish works, some without attribution. They included a *Madonna and child encircled by a garland of flowers* purported to be by Daniel Seghers, *An archery match* said to be by David Teniers the younger and a Flemish *Fruit piece*. These three were shown again at the recent Gallery opening.[2] The contribution of the Colonial Government was made up with two other oils, *The Guards leaving Gravesend, Feb. 19, 1885,* by the contemporary British marine painter, Charles Wyllie (1853-1923) and an Australian subject

piece *Woolshed, New South Wales,* by Godfrey Rivers. There were, in addition, seventy engravings, many 'after the antique', a number of loan watercolours and a single item of portrait sculpture.[3] A portrait (copy) of the Queen, also belonging to the Government, was included at the last moment.

The fact that practically all the major works shown had already been seen at earlier Brisbane exhibitions must have given the occasion a quality of extreme *déjà vu*. Yet the public of the 1890s were now able to boast of that indispensable ornament, an art collection on permanent display.

Contemporary opinion about the opening day was far from enthusiastic. Gasking, the *Queenslander's* illustrator, felt that the odds were against the whole thing. His cartoon shows Art as an 'aesthetic' Greek lady standing stalwart at the empty portal of some imagined gallery. Her proud gaze is concentrated well above the Philistine masses rushing to buy lottery tickets. The *Telegraph* editorial of the day following the opening sounded a similar pessimistic note.[4] Instead of praise for what was really the culmination of a decade of Brisbane's artistic hopes, the author dwells gloomily on what he felt was the 'low realism' of Australian art in general. In his opinion this was due largely to the monotonous colour of the landscape and the permanently warm weather. His sympathy lay instead with the European tradition and more lofty and idealized forms of artistic endeavour.

Despite this view, if we look at the actual works on display, we see that some attempt was made to cater to the requirement for idealized and uplifting works of art. The notion of the National Gallery as an establishment for the education and improvement of public taste had been, as was the case with so many nineteenth-century galleries, central to its development. Godfrey Rivers, a prominent English-trained artist and prime mover for the

formation of the Gallery, held firm views in this respect.[5] The fact that many of the idealized works on view were not originals but copies after Raphael and Botticelli, or engravings after Rubens and Poussin, was in no sense regarded as disadvantageous. It was simply an economic factor that had to be faced in the impoverished cultural life of the Colony. Indeed, contemporary photographs of the crowded display show that copies of works such as Raphael's *Madonna della Sedia*, loaned by the Honourable James Dickson, M.L.A., were prominently displayed by Rivers, who had organized the arrangements.

The nineteenth-century commonplace idea that public taste could be refined by contact with something generally accepted to be better had been the view of the former Colonial Governor, Sir Anthony Musgrave, a firm patron of the arts. Some eleven years before the National Gallery opened he was pressing for the establishment of a permanent gallery for Brisbane. Aware that the Colony was hardly likely to be able to afford many original works of art for such a gallery, he suggested that contributions by local collectors be augmented with copies and casts of well-known works of art.[6] To some degree, Musgrave's hopes were to be fulfilled.

Many of the oils on display in 1895 had been seen before at exhibitions of the Queensland Art Society or the National Association. The Association's Jubilee Exhibition of 1887 was of particular significance in this regard. Here an important work shown was Wyllie's *The Guards leaving Gravesend, Feb. 19, 1885*, a painting of the vessel S.S. *Manora*.[7] This painting was presented to the Colonial Government by the commercial firm, Gray Dawes and Co., probably in 1886.

In this year the managing agents of the Australian United Steam Navigation Co. Ltd, that included Gray Dawes & Co., had opened their Head Office in Brisbane and the gift was made on condition that it be part of the National Gallery when formed.[8] The painting had some topical interest as it is likely that the *Manora* was used by the British India Steam Navigation Company in the regular Queensland-Suez run.[9] The painting was exhibited again in 1892 before it found a temporary home in the National Gallery.

Godfrey Rivers's Riverina subject, *Woolshed, New South Wales*, 1890, the only Australian subject painting at the opening in 1895, had been also previously exhibited in Brisbane. It had been up for sale at the 1891 National Association display for £84.0.0 and, not finding a buyer, was later donated to the Gallery by the artist. It had been shown initially in 1890 at the Deanery in Sydney and

top and below
Photographs of the opening display in the *Queenslander*, 13 April 1895

CHARLES WYLLIE   THE GUARDS LEAVING GRAVESEND,
FEB. 19, 1885
Oil   91 × 51 cm
Presented by British India Steam Navigation Co. Ltd, 1895

has most unusual thematic similarities with Tom Roberts's *Shearing the rams* of the same year.

Several oils by Heinrich Gogarten were loaned to the 1887 Jubilee Exhibition by the Chief Justice Sir Samuel Griffith.[10] One of these, *Icebound on the Elbe,* the present whereabouts of which is unknown, was loaned again for the opening day of the National Gallery. Sir Samuel had a substantial interest in the idea of the Gallery and he was President of its first Board of Trustees. He appears to have bought, on behalf of the Colony, about two hundred engravings after the Old Masters with the idea of placing them on some sort of permanent display.[11] Little practical was done to make this possible until Godfrey Rivers made a definite proposal in 1894. The seventy engravings that were finally shown at the opening exhibition drew a mixed response but as a 'tolerably complete history of the art of engraving in Europe from the earliest time to the present day' they clearly had sound educational value.[12] At the time of the Jubilee Exhibition, too, a local photographer and entrepreneur, E.T.B. Hutchison, knowing of Griffith's interest in engravings, tried to sell him a number of steel engravings after biblical paintings by Gustave Doré. The sale did not go through but Hutchison presented seven to the Gallery for its opening display.[13]

From its first exhibition in 1888, the Queensland Art Society had seen itself in every way as a vital step in the progress toward the eventual formation of a national gallery. By the August exhibition of 1893, Rivers, as President, noted in his opening speech that significant steps had been taken to form the National Gallery.[14] The move was made despite a refusal in 1892 by the Art Galllery of New South Wales to loan pictures. Yet Brisbane was in the throes of a financial depression that made any definite proposal unacceptable. Nevertheless, the economic situation did little to spoil the Society's 1893 exhibition. The works were wide in range and included items by Tom Roberts, John Mather and Arthur Streeton. Oscar Friström also showed his curiously detailed, posthumous portrait of the aged 'identity' James Davies, *Durramboi.* Isaac Jenner who, despite claims to the contrary, seems to have had little concrete to do with the Gallery, exhibited his strikingly romantic seascape *Cape Chudleigh, Labrador,* 1890, with its gigantic icy floes and minute penguins. These two works were presented to the National Gallery, not for the opening day, but with several others immediately afterward.[15] It is possible that the gifts were made to counter that of Godfrey Rivers whose dominating personality in Brisbane's art world was certainly an irritation to Friström at this time. Jenner's painting was offered to the people of Queensland as the nearest thing to an appropriate history

painting, for the subject was connected with the life of the Arctic explorer Sir John Franklin, who had had some slight association with Australia.[16]

Perhaps the most noteworthy aspect of the 1893 Society exhibition was the presence of the Murray-Prior loan collection. This was offered to the Government four months later for the express purpose of forming the nucleus of the Gallery.[17] The offer was not immediately taken up yet the value of these works was shrewdly assessed by one exhibition critic. He felt that they were in some respects something that Queensland artists could aspire to but, more importantly, 'they should serve to rid us of the European legend and make us aware that the nineteenth century and this colony of Queensland have after all something to say for themselves'.[18] For some, at least, the Old Masters had, by default, a role to play in Australian art.

On 18 September, 1894, Godfrey Rivers sent to the Government a full proposal for an art gallery.[19] In brief, Rivers noted that the Government was already in possession of a number of fine engravings, which, he claimed, were lying in the cellars of the Treasury Building and gradually deteriorating. He suggested in his proposal that about fifty be mounted and framed and together with Wyllie's painting, a so-called Titian owned by the Government and a loan collection, the gallery could be started. He suggested, too, the appointment of three to four trustees and the necessity of a well-lit central room, offering his services to collect money, to select loans and to superintend the gallery.[20] Rivers, who had close contacts in Sydney, may well have seen himself in an artistic role similar to Julian Ashton, who was both a teacher and closely involved with the workings of the New South Wales Art Gallery.

No doubt as a result of Rivers's scheme, the renewed offer of her husband's paintings by Mrs Prior was accepted by the Government shortly afterward, and money was put aside to frame the engravings. The Government also informed Rivers that a room would be set apart as a temporary art gallery, the public to be admitted on the order of the Speaker.[21] Brisbane's first official art gallery was, in fact, not the Town Hall, but a committee room in the new wing of the Parliament House. By November 1894 all one needed to see the displayed works was a pass from the Speaker.[22]

Transferred to the Town Hall, the collection of the National Gallery was ready for permanent display. For the opening day the walls were especially repainted in neutral tints and movable screens were supplied to minimize the size of the room. In a lengthy article in the *Queenslander*, the full extent of the collection and the loan items is described.[23] It is perhaps to the journalist's credit that although he discusses the copies of Old Masters and the engravings after Poussin, Rembrandt and Rubens, he gives priority of his copy to Charles Wyllie's contemporary sea piece, *The Guards leaving Gravesend, Feb. 19, 1885*. Here, he claimed, was the shining example of the power of art over unpromising material. The perspective was cleverly managed and a delight, and the skilful grouping and harmonious atmosphere of the whole made an abiding pleasure. One could scarcely ever weary of such a picture.

Unfortunately, today's visitors do not have the opportunity of evaluating this work, which was central to the National Gallery's first display in 1895, for it no longer forms part of the Queensland Art Gallery's Collection.[24] Sadly, too, no attempt was made to present even a small tribute to the Gallery's first collection at the 1982 July opening extravaganza.

ISAAC WALTER JENNER   CAPE CHUDLEIGH, LABRADOR
1890
Oil on canvas on composition board
76 × 127cm
Gift of the artist, 1895

[1] *Queenslander*, 6 April 1895. The Western Australian Art Gallery, however, opened on 31 July, 1895.

[2] *The Illustrated Catalogue of the Queensland National Art Gallery*, Brisbane, 1908, lists only seven paintings in the Murray-Prior Bequest. The three paintings shown in 1982 have as yet not been fully authenticated.

[3] Some of the most interesting watercolours were *Sandgate Pier* by Robert Rayment, a local artist, three David Cox landscapes, and three small scenery studies by the New Zealand painter, Peerless. The landscapes purporting to be by the English painter, David Cox (father or son) were entitled *An avenue, Showery weather*, and *A homestead*, and were loaned by Henry Oxley, an important local art patron.

[4] *Telegraph*, 30 March 1895.

[5] These views were put forward in his Presidential speech marking the opening of the 1892 Art Society exhibition. Rivers (1859-1925), who had trained at the Slade under Legros, was Art Master at the Brisbane Technical College.

[6] *Brisbane Courier*, 19 July 1884.

[7] The title in the catalogue reads rather differently but other evidence confirms it to be Wyllie's painting of the S.S. *Manora*. The S.S. *Manora* departed with troops from Gravesend on 19 February, 1885, bound for Suakin in the Sudan. An Australian battalion and battery took part in the fighting at Suakin.

[8] *Brisbane Courier*, 30 March 1895.

[9] G. Blake, *B.I. Centenary: The Story of the British India Steam Navigation Co. Ltd., 1956*. See also N. Pixley 'History of the A.U.S.N. Co. Ltd., and its Predecessors', *Journal of the Historical Society of Queensland*, Vol. 5, No. 2, 1954.

[10] Heinrich Gogarten (1850-1911), German-trained at Dusseldorf, mainly a painter of winter landscapes.

[11] *Queenslander*, 6 April 1895.

[12] *Brisbane Courier*, 30 March 1895.

[13] Hutchison exhibited six of the engravings including a *Massacre of the innocents*, *Christ's entry into Jerusalem*, and *Pilate's wife's dream* at the Jubilee Exhibition.
    The following year Hutchison tried to sell a further number of these engravings at a Grand Art union. See the full discussion in J. Brown and M. Maynard 'Painter and Photographer: Brisbane in the 1880's and 1890's', *History of Photography*, October 1978.

[14] *Queenslander*, 19 August 1893.

[15] *Queenslander*, 13 April 1895.

[16] Letter of donation written by Jenner. Queensland Art Gallery archives.

[17] Letter to Mrs Murray-Prior from the Assistant Under-Secretary dated 2 November 1894, *Queensland State Archives*.

[18] *Queenslander*, 19 August 1893.

[19] The entire proposal scheme from Rivers is held by the *Queensland State Archives*. This information was made available to the Trustees of the Art Gallery of New South Wales almost immediately afterward.

[20] Rivers discharged the duties of a Curator and acted as Honorary Secretary to the Trustees of the Gallery from the time of its establishment. He was officially appointed Curator without salary only in October 1898. Letter from the Colonial Under-Secretary to Rivers, 17 October 1898, *Queensland State Archives*.

[21] Verbal message from Mr Nelson to Rivers on 15 November 1894, recorded in correspondence, *Queensland State Archives*.

[22] *Brisbane Courier*, 16 November 1894.

[23] *Queenslander*, 6 April 1895.

[24] This painting is now in the collection of P & O Australia Ltd, Sydney.

Artist's choice no. 14

Russell Drysdale:
Man feeding his dogs *by Davida Allen*

Looking at pictures — maybe it's got a lot to do with seeing images that trigger off something in the viewer. *The bathers* are at my creek! It's the same creek that we have on our land. It is the same when you meet someone — you have to feel there is a cord of similarity somewhere. Maybe the string gets pulled when the stranger relates an experience that you, too, have undergone — interest is triggered off; so, when I saw Arthur Streeton's *The bathers*, there was my creek; there were my gum-trees. Funnily enough, for probably the same reason, Russell Drysdale's *Man feeding his dogs*, 1941, 'got to me'!

My husband had two bull-terriers. The mad, loyalty-bond I watched him develop with those stupid, non-human animals surged up in me strangely and strongly. The lean man, the lean dogs — a physical bond visually. (If I had been Russell Drysdale I'd have used exactly the same technique of bonding man and dog!)

As I was captured by *Man feeding his dogs*, there suddenly appeared the most extraordinary, peculiar chair, drawn hanging on one of the dead tree's dead stub branches. My first thoughts were 'oh, how delightful but what the hell . . .' then the scale phenomenon hit me worryingly. It is a chair out of place. The man could not possibly sit on it but the other figure, leaning against a tree in the background, might have a better chance at sitting on it — and yet, visually, it's not meant for him either. If that chair were not there, this lovely little painting (51.2 × 61.4 cm) could settle in one of my neat mental drawers and collect time's cobwebs; but Drysdale, the artist, has vehicled a disturbing reality in this space which I cannot closet!

The dogs are hungry. One of them is rearing up for his meat in the bag. The right-hand, sitting-down dog could nip or maim. The man leaning against the tree in the background has an Australian, lazy, 'get a bloody move on' look and he reinforces the Surrealism of the chair's presence — why is he there, looking at the man feeding his dogs? He can see the chair in front of him and yet he doesn't seem to give a damn! His acceptance of it, stuck up on that stub of a branch, demands that I, as casually, accept it too — but I cannot!! My life had been moved, redirected by a stick-drawn, bentwood chair stuck in a tree. I wallowed in the absurdity of it all.

Two hours later, I found myself spilling over with my enthusiasm for my find at a table of several people. One man listened attentively but spoke destructively, with reason.

'It's a flooded landscape' — he had pronounced the sentence of death to all my dreams.

'Yes, the chair is there because of previous devastation — the clue to a flooded landscape.'

I struggled with the starkness of reason. I did not want to know any reason for its existence. The dog rearing to maim — the tenseness of his front feet, looking flat on the ground but energy there, ready to rear up with an electric pounce at the bag of meat . . . one dog already in the electric leap . . . the man's wiry body containing the same pulse . . . trees not echoing but screeching out horridly with empathy.

'No, Hamish!!' I yelled at my executioner.

'A chair in a tree — an obvious natural consequence.'

'But I have *seen* the painting! No; I will not accept the flood. There is too much at stake.'

Davida Allen is an expressive, figurative painter who lives and works in Queensland.

RUSSELL DRYSDALE   MAN FEEDING HIS DOGS   1941
Oil on canvas   51 × 61 cm
Gift of C. F. Viner-Hall, 1961

European art

by Gertrude Langer

HENRI DE TOULOUSE-LAUTREC   TETE DE FILLE   1892
Oil on wood   28 × 24 cm
Purchased 1959. Major Harold de Vahl Rubin Gift

Gertrude Langer, O.B.E., Ph.D. (Art History), is art critic for the Brisbane Courier-Mail. She has honorary life membership of the Queensland Arts Council and the Arts Council of Australia and is patron of the Institute of Modern Art, Brisbane, and the Brisbane Art School.

The collection of European art in the Queensland Art Gallery is not large but includes paintings, sculptures and graphic works of importance.

Lack of funds and, until very recently, even of a proper home to house valuable works, have been major problems.

Prior to the establishment of the Queensland Art Gallery Foundation in 1980, the Gallery owned only a few pre-nineteenth-century paintings, mainly of Netherlandish origin, none of them of major importance. One may mention a seventeenth-century Flemish *Madonna with child encircled by a garland of flowers* and a genre scene depicting *An archery match,* attributed to David Teniers, the younger. Some more important works other than paintings will be mentioned later.

The first work purchased through the Queensland Art Gallery Foundation was a late Gothic panel painting by the Netherlandish Master of Frankfurt, 1460-1520/30, so-called because he executed altarpieces for that German city. The picture, *c.* 1496, shows *Virgin and Child with Saint James the Pilgrim, Saint Catherine and the Donor with Saint Peter.*

Max Friedländer, well-known expert in early Netherlandish art, I understand made the attribution. In his estimation (see his book *Von Eyck bis Bruegel, Verlag Julius Bard Berlin,* 1921), the Master of Frankfurt borrowed much from other Netherlandish painters. The painting in the Gallery shows a typical subject in a manner typical of the late Gothic period. However, there are disturbing elements: there is a lot of finely executed detail, some symbolic, some homely, but the composition lacks formal cohesion; there are gaucheries in the handling of the figures not found in good Netherlandish paintings of that century, and there are great discrepancies in the relative head-sizes of the figures. X-ray examination carried out in Brisbane revealed that alterations had been made — presumably during the lifetime of the artist — in the final version, the most interesting being the change of the original donatrix into a male donor. As is, the donor has a strikingly individual face with an intense expression.

Before the opening of the new Gallery great efforts were made to acquire major works of art. Peter Paul Rubens's copy of Titian's *Girl in a fur* in the Vienna Kunsthistorisches Museum is such a work. (Prior to its acquisition by the Gallery, the painting suffered damage in a car accident and had to undergo restoration before arriving at its Queensland resting place.) One of many copies Rubens made after the revered master, it is believed by some that Rubens first saw Titian's *Girl in a fur* when he was in London on a diplomatic mission; the painting then was in the collection of King Charles I. Comparison of the Rubens copy with the original clearly shows how subtle changes in the nuances of features and expression transformed the Italian beauty into an approximation of Rubens's own ideal woman.

It has been pointed out that the Titian portrait probably also inspired Rubens's famous portrait of *Hélene Fourment with fur,* also in the Vienna Kunsthistorisches.

Rubens's greatest pupil, Anthony van Dyck, is now also represented in the Queensland Gallery. His full-length *Portrait of the Marchese Filippo Spinola* (he was the son of the Commander at the surrender of Breda, an event immortalized in Velasquez's magnificent painting) belongs to van Dyck's Genoese period, when the brilliant young master had many portrait commissions from Italian nobles.

Executed *c.* 1622-27, the portrait of the Marchese lacks the expression of neurasthenic languor, sometimes bordering on affectation, characteristic of later van Dycks. The unassuming noblesse of bearing of the youngish man in armour reminds one of Titian's portraits, and it is known that while in Italy, van Dyck adapted to Italian taste, as his master, Rubens, had done two decades before. The Titian-Rubens trappings (columns and rich, crimson curtain) create an impression of grandeur; the agitation of the curtain introduces an element of drama into the otherwise calm structure of the painting. The painting technique is of great finesse.

The Resurrection by Tintoretto, *c.* 1550, is a newly discovered early work by the great Venetian. Tintoretto scholar, Paola Rossi, supported her attribution by pointing out the similarity of the Christ figure in this painting to the one in a much later Tintoretto, the *Descent into limbo,* for San Cassiano, and also to a Tintoretto drawing. I can only rely on material on *The Resurrection* made available to me by the Gallery staff, more thorough research being beyond the scope and time allowed for this article. However, I venture to remark that *The Resurrection,* which does not yet show the 'eccentricities' of Tintoretto's developed style, might be typical of the young artist's initial ambition to combine Michelangelo's plastic values with Titian's colour. It seems that Tintoretto was eager to show off, in the figure of Christ, his fluent handling of the difficult contrapposto. He brought off also an effective synthesis of drama and calm, as seen in the axial structure of the painting — the contrasts of light and dark, and warm and cool colours — and, while giving the body of Christ a rather pagan-sensual treatment, did not lose altogether the spirituality of the event. (When it comes to the victory of spirituality over the flesh, we have to think of El Greco, who learned from Tintoretto.)

To the same period belongs one of the Gallery's most prized possessions, the red wax relief depicting *The flagellation of Christ* by Giovanni Bologna (or Giambologna or Jean de Boulogne), who lived from 1525 to 1608. Born in Douai and trained in Flanders, he became, after the death of Michelangelo, the most famed sculptor in Italy. (Giambologna's *Mercury,* poised on one toe in a movement of flight, is probably his most reproduced work.)

The relief of *The flagellation of Christ* is one

below
MASTER OF FRANKFURT   VIRGIN AND CHILD WITH SAINT JAMES THE PILGRIM, SAINT CATHERINE AND THE DONOR WITH SAINT PETER   *c.*1496
Egg tempera or a tempera emulsion on a gesso ground on oak panel   69 × 50cm
Purchased 1980. Queensland Art Gallery Foundation with funds from the Utah Foundation

above
GIAMBOLOGNA   THE FLAGELLATION OF CHRIST
*c.*1579
(Study for a bronze panel)
Red wax relief on a wooden ground
48 × 74 × 10cm
Gift of the Queensland Museum, 1965

above
EDOUARD VUILLARD   LE SALON DES
HESSEL   c.1906
Oil on canvas   180 × 382 cm
Purchased 1981..Queensland Art Gallery
Foundation   ©S.P.A.D.E.M. Paris, 1983

left
MAURICE DE VLAMINCK   NATURE MORTE
Oil on canvas   33 × 41 cm
Purchased 1959. Major Harold de Vahl Rubin
Gift   ©S.P.A.D.E.M. Paris, 1983

PABLO PICASSO   FEMME AU PARASOL COUCHEE
SUR LA PLAGE   1933
Gouache, wash, pen and indian ink on wove paper
40 × 51 cm
Purchased 1959. Major Harold de Vahl Rubin Gift
© S.P.A.D.E.M. Paris, 1983

of six wax reliefs for casting in bronze for the Grimaldi Chapel in Genoa. It was handed over to the Queensland Art Gallery in 1965 after it had been accidentally discovered in the basement of the Queensland Museum. Three of the other wax reliefs are in the Victoria and Albert Museum, London.

Fitting in with this group of works is the bronze, *Hercules and Omphale, c.* 1700, by Giovanni Battista Foggini, acquired in 1980. The finely detailed work, with its complex rhythms, is designed to offer a variety of satisfying silhouettes. Foggini was the outstanding sculptor and decorator in the 'twilight-period' of the Florence of the Medici.

In 1959, during the directorship of Robert Haines, the Queensland Art Gallery received a most exciting gift from Major Harold de Vahl Rubin, comprising three Picassos, a Degas, a Renoir, a Toulouse-Lautrec and a Vlaminck. This gift has since become the nucleus around which paintings, bronzes and prints have been gathered.

Central to the gift is Picasso's *La belle hollandaise,* one of those works that has a radiance. The radiance emanates from the young woman, realized by Picasso as solid and self-contained as a carving in stone, yet as warmly human and erotic as life itself. The inscription tells that Picasso did this work in Holland in 1905 and gave it to his friend, Paco Durio. In 1980 it was lent by the Gallery to the Museum of Modern Art for its Picasso retrospective.

In 1908-09, excited by the combined impact of Cézanne and primitive sculpture, Picasso did a number of heads, similar to *Tête d'homme,* which is held in the Queensland Gallery. Most similarly constructed is a head done in gouache I found reproduced in D.D. Duncan's *Picasso's Picassos.* Coming soon after *Les demoiselles d'Avignon, Tête d'homme,* too, is a good example of the first, formative phase of Cubism.

Femme au parasol couchée sur la plage is an example of those astonishing re-creations of the human form Picasso had begun to draw at Cannes. The dislocations are convincing organically, as well as emotionally, and one marvels at this blend of horror, humour and majestic calm. The woman, poised against the sea, seems to be transformed into a shell-creature. Did the people go on with their daily pleasures while clouds gathered over Europe?

above
JEAN BAPTISTE CAMILLE COROT   ENVIRONS DE ROME
1866   (First state of three)
Etching on cream laid paper with watermark   29 × 21 cm
Purchased 1979

below
JEAN-FRANCOIS MILLET   LA BARATTEUSE   1885
Etching on thin ivory laid paper   18 × 12 cm
Gift of Mrs Lillian Bosch, 1977

Is it this Picasso wanted to say? The year is 1933.

Degas and Toulouse-Lautrec were early influences on Picasso. In *Trois danseuses à la classe de danse,* we have one of the most favoured themes of Degas, dancers captured in casual off-stage poses. The painting shows his impeccable sense of composition (in the new Japanese-influenced manner) and draughtsmanship. The soft shimmer of the painting is achieved partly by the use of cardboard as ground.

Tête de fille by Henri de Toulouse-Lautrec is one of sixteen medallions painted by Lautrec in 1892 for a 'maison close' in Paris. It is remarkable how much he says with a bit of flat, opaque paint and those sparse, fluent, transparent contour lines and strokes. Quite an essence of Lautrec's art is distilled in this tiny oil.

Nature morte, by Maurice de Vlaminck, I would date between 1908 and 1910, which is Vlaminck's 'Cézannesque' period. Like many artists at the time, Vlaminck had fallen under the spell of the Cézanne Retrospective, 1907, in Paris. He abandoned his loud *Fauve* colours and concentrated on simplified form and tilted planes. Soon after this interlude, he consolidated the style, free of theories, by which he is best known.

Renoir's portrait of his little children, *Coco et Jean,* is a tender painting of the artist's later years when, plagued by rheumatism, he had been forced to move permanently to Cagnes on the Mediterranean. Using transparent oils and the dominating reds of his late period, the forms, under a caressing brush, reach the bloom and delicacy of flower petals. Their faces averted from the viewer, the children are withdrawn into their own world.

Added to the collection of French paintings was the small oil, *La lessive à Eragny* by Camille Pissarro, as well as a luminously painted apple orchard by Gustave Loiseau (following closely in the footsteps of Monet) and two Breton landscapes by Henri Moret and Maxime Maufra. Loiseau, Moret and Maufra all belonged to the group around Gauguin at Pont-Aven, Brittany, but all three, and particularly Loiseau, remained more or less Impressionists.

The purchase last year of Edouard Vuillard's large canvas, *Le salon des Hessel,* c. 1906, was a major event for the Gallery. In

right
PIERRE AUGUSTE RENOIR   COCO ET JEAN
c. 1904-05
Oil on canvas   31 × 42 cm
Purchased 1959. Major Harold de Vahl Rubin
Gift

below
PAUL CEZANNE   LES GRANDS BAIGNEURS
c. 1896-98
(Second state of three)
Colour lithograph on laid paper with watermark   41 × 51 cm
Purchased 1981

left
TINTORETTO　　THE RESURRECTION　　*c.*1550s
Oil on canvas　　201 × 139cm
Purchased 1981. Queensland Art Gallery Foundation

below left
ANTHONY VAN DYCK　　PORTRAIT OF THE MARCHESE
FILIPPO SPINOLA　　*c.*1622-27
Oil on canvas　　218 × 140cm
Purchased 1981. Queensland Art Gallery Foundation

below
PETER PAUL RUBENS　　PORTRAIT OF A YOUNG WOMAN
IN A FUR WRAP　　*c.*1629-30
(After Titian's *Girl in a fur*)
Oil on canvas　　92 × 68cm
Purchased 1980. Queensland Art Gallery Foundation

PABLO PICASSO   TETE D'HOMME   c. 1906-07
Pencil and watercolour wash on wove paper   31 × 24 cm
Purchased 1959. Major Harold de Vahl Rubin Gift
© S.P.A.D.E.M. Paris, 1983

AUGUSTE RODIN   THE ACROBAT
Bronze   29 × 15 × 13cm
Purchased 1960. Alderman and Mrs J. B.
Chandler Citizens Appreciation Fund

spite of his Intimism, Vuillard liked expanding over wide formats. His talent was well suited to murals (he did some), and the application of colour and mattness, suggestive of tapestry, demonstrated by *Le salon des Hessel*, seems to indicate that he would have been a marvellous designer for tapestries, had he been given the chance. Apart from his mother, with whom he lived until her death at the age of ninety, Madame Hessel was Vuillard's greatest friend and inspiration. *Le salon des Hessel* is a magic painting. The hushed, autumnal colour scheme, which includes bare patches of unprimed canvas, the reddish light of end of day, the dematerialized figures and objects, which are woven into the rhythms of the picture — all that and something intangible — create a nostalgic, lingering mood, as if the painting had arisen from a Proustian *À la recherche du temps perdu*. The painting came from the Vuillard Estate, Paris, and like other works from the Estate seems to have remained unfinished; but, if so, this only increases the mood of mystery and transitoriness.

The Gallery owns an important group of bronzes supplementing the French paintings. There are four bronzes by Rodin, including *Crouching woman* and *The acrobat*, which is one of those small, now so much appreciated sculptures that just 'grew' under Rodin's hands and speak directly as vital forms.

The artist whose sculpture is closest to Rodin in the study of movement is Degas. Rodin admired his small wax and clay models, which were never cast during Degas's lifetime. The Gallery owns *The dancer*, cast from the wax model after the artist's death, as well as a bronze cast of his *Portrait study of Madame S*.

Of Rodin's most important co-worker, Antoine Bourdelle, the Gallery holds the expressively modelled bust of *Madame Bourdelle*. The enchanting bronze of *Madame Renoir* by Renoir speaks of the fullness of life, as does Picasso's *La belle hollandaise*.

Representing Charles Despiau, who worked for several years in Rodin's studio, is a smaller version of his Neo-classical *Apollo*. A recently acquired bronze cast from Paul Gauguin's plaster sculpture of *Madame Schuffenecker* (wife of the man who introduced Gauguin to the basics of painting) is a charming portrait in a conventional style not usually associated with Gauguin. *Le génie de la danse, c.*1865, is a small version of the central figure of Jean-Baptiste Carpeaux's group on the façade of the Paris Opera. When unveiled, this sculpture caused a public outcry because of the unclassical 'impure' nudes. The piece in the Gallery is an excellent cast.

Jules Aimé Dalou was a pupil of Carpeaux, who introduced him to Rodin. The bronze, *Wisdom supporting Liberty*, 1889, acquired in 1982, is the finished study for the right-hand group of Dalou's monument to Leon Gambetta. The plaster model of the piece is in the collection of the Petit Palais, Paris. Of course, one must not omit to mention an interesting over-life-size bronze, *Bather*, by the contemporary Italian sculptor, Emilio Greco. The sculpture looks well in the Water Mall of the Gallery. Across the centuries, this heir of the elongated figures in complex poses typical of Italian Mannerism, links up with the examples of that period in our Gallery.

Only late in the day, and when drawings and prints by the famous had become very expensive, the Gallery turned its attention to building up a collection of graphic works and adding to the scant existing holdings. Although the European graphics are very inadequate in number, many are of high quality, both in terms of technique and of artistic merit. They include a few etchings by Rembrandt, about nine woodcuts of Durer's 'Apocalypse', a squared-up drawing of the *Last Supper* by Jean Cousin the elder (sixteenth century), a chalk drawing of *Venus with two amoretti* by François Boucher, a fine seventeenth-century hand-drawing of a landscape by Jan van Goyen, and a few other earlier graphics.

From the nineteenth and twentieth centuries the Gallery holds an impressive lithograph by Géricault, the very beautiful *Environs de Rome* by Corot, and *La toilette* by Manet, who was known to be a superb etcher. The etching *La baratteuse*, by Jean-François Millet, celebrates the dignity of humble work by means of a dignified composition, as does the splendid etching by Camille Pissarro, depicting haymakers.

Symbolism is represented by Redon's *Centaur aiming at the clouds*; Gauguin's litho-

graphs *Watched by the spirit of the dead* and *Old Women, Arles;* Munch's *Madonna* (we remember that Munch did his first prints in Paris where he was influenced by Gauguin); four etchings/aquatints by Rouault, including one in colour; James Ensor's hand-coloured etching, *Pride,* from his album *The seven deadly sins,* and two early woodcuts from his *Klänge,* by Kandinsky. The Gallery is glad also of a lovely colour lithograph from Vuillard's *Interieurs et paysages* and Bonnard's delicious *Women with umbrella.*

Nu au fauteuil, les bras levés, one of Matisse's more classically inclined works of the early 1920s is, of course, quite inadequate as the only example of his genius; also, there is only one etching by Braque. Further prints include the etching *Buste* by Giacometti, *Death and the artist,* by Lovis Corinth, from his folio Totentanz, some etchings by Käthe Kollwitz and Liebermann's etching of Gerhart Hauptmann. One of the most precious possessions among graphics is Cézanne's colour lithograph (printed by Auguste Clot), *Les grands baigneurs.* Cézanne did only three lithographs in his life, which were commissioned by his dealer, Ambroise Vollard. Although the lithograph in question is based on a much earlier painting, it shows far greater strength of composition. This work is the only Cézanne in the Gallery and is especially important because it shows a perfect solution of a theme which occupied Cézanne during his whole life, namely the relationship of nudes and the landscape. The landscape in *Les grands baigneurs* also includes *Le Mont Ste Victoire,* held almost sacred by Cézanne.

The Gallery's European holdings contain few Abstract works. Not all can be mentioned, but attention is drawn to Laszlo Moholy-Nagy's *Prehistoric Construction,* 1942 (oil on incised transparent synthetic polymer resin mounted in an original shadow-box frame), to an exciting tapestry, *Syncopée,* designed by Sonia Delaunay and woven in Aubusson by the master weaver, Filibert Pinton (donated by the Queensland Art Gallery Society to mark the opening of the new Gallery) and to a small number of modern Abstract prints, including serigraphs by Vasarely, Dorazio, and a colour etching, aquatint, by Sonia Delaunay.

left
EMILIO GRECO   BATHER   1956
Bronze   218 cm high (with base)
Purchased 1966

below
CAMILLE PISSARRO   FANEUSE D'ERAGNY   1897
(from *Art of Nature*)
Etching   32 × 25 cm
Purchased 1980

Recent acquisitions by public galleries

above
FRED WILLIAMS   ECHUCA LANDSCAPE   1961
Oil on composition board   122 × 143cm
Purchased 1982. Queensland Art Gallery Foundation

Echuca landscape is the Queensland Art Gallery's major
Australian acquisition for 1982. Painted in 1961, it was one
result of a 1958-59 trip to the Barmah and Echuca forests in
Nothern Victoria by Fred Williams and Arthur Boyd. It is
a particularly rich and gripping painting from the artist's early
Cubist series. The Gallery is fortunate in possessing the
related etching *Echuca landscape*, gifted by the artist's widow
in 1982.

left
JEAN BAPTISTE CARPEAUX   GENIUS OF THE DANCE
c.1865
Bronze   55cm high
Purchased 1982. Queensland Art Gallery Foundation

The baroque inspiration and high finish of *Genius of the dance*
is indicative of the style which gained Jean Baptiste Carpeaux
the stature of leading French sculptor of the mid-nineteenth
century.
This bronze is taken from the central figure of a group
commissioned by the Paris Opera in 1865.

above
WILLIAM DELAFIELD COOK   A HAYSTACK   1982
Synthetic polymer paint on canvas   183 × 305cm
Purchased 1982. Queensland Art Gallery Foundation

A haystack is a very fine example by William Delafield Cook
of that realism which transcends photography. The primary
focus is on the mass of straw, painstakingly drawn and painted
with fine sable brushes. In this painting, the artist's technical
dexterity and success with the intricacies of perspective
are obvious.

right
JULES AIME DALOU   WISDOM SUPPORTING LIBERTY
1889
Bronze   60cm high
Purchased 1982. Queensland Art Gallery Foundation

Jules Aime Dalou was, with Rodin, a student of Carpeaux.
His naturalism is often tempered with allegory, as in the recently
acquired bronze, *Wisdom supporting liberty*. This model,
dating from 1889, was incorporated into a group on
the monument to Leon Gambetta in Bordeaux.

British art

by Caroline Launitz-Schurer

JOHN OPIE   SELF PORTRAIT   c.1780s
Oil on canvas   54 × 43cm
Purchased 1952. Miss Maria Therese Treweeke Bequest

Caroline Launitz-Schurer, M.A., is Assistant Director of the Queensland Art Gallery. She is currently writing her doctoral thesis on nineteenth-century American cultural history, and is particularly interested in American art of the nineteenth and twentieth centuries.

The first work purchased in 1896 by the newly established Queensland Art Gallery was *Evicted,* by the British artist, Blandford Fletcher. The painting, which had been exhibited at the Royal Academy and at the Chicago Columbian Exposition, cost 300 guineas at a time when the annual Government grant was £550. It is hardly surprising that the Gallery's first purchase should be a British work. At the turn of the century, Britain was the standard by which Australian society judged what was important in cultural and intellectual life.

One could argue that the British collections of all Australian galleries, until as late as the 1950s, provide a valuable insight into the 'self-image' of the different Australian States. As the Queensland Gallery's first purchase, *Evicted* is significant because of its Victorian social-conscience theme.[1] Indeed, one is struck by the emphasis on serious narrative, genre and landscape in the paintings in the British collection to 1908. There was an absence of the flamboyant and grandiose Neo-classical and historical subjects favoured by the Sydney and Melbourne galleries at the same time.

However, a surprising number of good works were purchased in the first ten years by a Gallery with only an Honorary Curator and limited funds.

The second major period for the development of the British collection came in the 1950s, when Robert Haines was the Director. During his directorship the Gallery acquired some excellent works by modern British artists, reflecting important developments in British art in the twentieth century. Works by Philip Wilson Steer, Walter Sickert, Harold Gilman, Spencer Gore, Lucien Pissarro, Augustus John, Matthew Smith, Bernard Meninsky, Stanley Spencer and Jacob Epstein

all entered the Collection in the 1950s.

More recently, the Gallery has added to the strength of its British collection with the purchase of some fine eighteenth-century portraits by Reynolds, Ramsay and Raeburn, by works on paper (including works by Gainsborough, J. M. W. Turner, and Samuel Palmer) and by augmenting the British watercolour collection. The latter collection includes works by Paul Sandby, John Cotman, David Cox, Richard Bonington, Russell Flint and Paul Nash.

In art-historical terms the earliest area of strength in the Queensland Art Gallery's British collection is the seventeenth-century and eighteenth-century British portrait collection, including a portrait attributed to Peter Lely, a work from the School of Thomas Hudson, a penetrating early *Self portrait* by 'the Cornish Wonder' John Opie, Thomas Gainsborough's *John Smith Esq., Clerk to the Drapers Company,* 1787, and Joshua Reynolds's *Portrait of Aneas Mackay of Ravenshead House.* However, it is the two Scottish artists, Allan Ramsay and Henry Raeburn, who gained a national reputation and whose works are the best examples of eighteenth-century portraits in the collection.

Allan Ramsay is represented by the fine early *Portrait of William Foster.* This was painted in 1741, soon after Ramsay's return from a period of study in Italy under Imperiali and Solimena; perhaps something of this Italian influence appears in the slightly European stance and look of the young Englishman.

Outstanding among the eighteenth-century portraits are two works by Henry Raeburn, *Portrait of Major-General Alexander Murray MacGregor as a young man,* and *Portrait of Lady Campbell,* both *c.* 1795. Raeburn was at his best painting men and the former

work typifies his greatest achievements in portraiture.

The eighteenth-century British collection also contains Angelica Kauffman's *The deserted Costanza* and a small work on panel attributed to Francis Wheatley, *The fish sellers*.

The nineteenth-century British collection is overwhelmingly Victorian and largely entered the Collection in the first few years after the Gallery was established. The exception is Edward Burne-Jones's lyrical and lovely *Aurora* of 1896, purchased in 1954. The influence of Botticelli in the figure of *Aurora*, who personifies the pre-Raphaelite ideal of female beauty, is typical of Burne-Jones's later work.

Among the most interesting of the Victorian narrative paintings are Philip Calderon's *Elizabeth Woodville, widow of Edward IV, parting with her younger son, the Duke of York*, Frederick Goodall's *The Holy Mother*, and Blandford

Fletcher's *Evicted*. The realism of *Evicted* compares well today with more purely sentimental Victorian works such as John Faed's *Annie tryst* or Robert Herdman's *Girl with a bundle of straw*, and contrasts with the almost pastoral qualities of Charles Martin Hardie's *The gleaners*. Napier Hemy's *The home wind* is reminiscent of Winslow Homer, but lacks the monumentality and psychological tension of the American artist's vision of men and the sea.

Nineteenth-century British landscapes include a fine John Glover *The confluence of the Machno and Conway Rivers (Wales)*, and a romantic Scottish landscape by D. Y. Cameron, *The everlasting hills*. Other Victorian works worth noting are Stanhope Forbes's *Village industry* (by an artist of the Newlyn School). Hamilton Macallum's *Sunday afternoon parade*, Harold Knight's *A cup of tea*, F. Cadogan's Cowper's late pre-Raphaelite *Hamlet*

BLANDFORD FLETCHER   EVICTED   1887
Oil on canvas   122 × 185 cm
Purchased 1896

This was the first work purchased by the Gallery

— *the churchyard scene*, and Alfred Gilbert's bronze *Perseus arming*.

The twentieth-century paintings, however, are the real strength of the British collection. Representative work by Frank Brangwyn and George Clausen's elegant *The Maiden* contrast with the Whistlerian influence obvious in Walter Greaves's *Thames, winter* and Philip Wilson Steer's *Battersea Reach*. The latter was painted in 1924 when Steer was moving closer to a fluid watercolour technique and when there are influences of Turner and Monet as well as Whistler in his work.[2]

Among artists who formed the Camden Town Group, Harold Gilman's *Clarissa (Nude)*, 1911-12, is a subtle and harmonious study and Walter Sickert's *Little Rachel* is part

above
BERNARD MENINSKY   PORTRAIT (Head of a girl)
c.1940s
Oil on canvas   51 × 41 cm
Purchased 1958

left
MATTHEW SMITH   GIRL IN YELLOW (Head and shoulders
of a girl)
Oil on canvas   51 × 41 cm
Purchased 1956. Beatrice Ethel Mallalieu Bequest

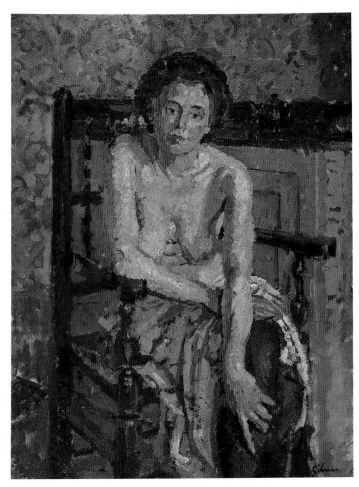

right
HAROLD GILMAN   CLARISSA (NUDE)   *c.*1911-12
Oil on canvas   61 × 46cm
Purchased 1956. Beatrice Ethel Mallalieu Bequest

below
WALTER RICHARD SICKERT   LITTLE RACHEL   1907
Oil on canvas   61 × 51cm
Purchased 1956 with the assistance of the National Gallery
Society

left
PHILIP WILSON STEER   BATTERSEA REACH   1924
Oil on canvas   38 × 69cm
Purchased 1958

below left
CHARLES NAPIER HEMY   THE HOME WIND   1901
Oil on canvas   123 × 184cm
Purchased 1903

below
ALFRED GILBERT   PERSEUS ARMING   c.1882
Bronze   69cm high
Gift of the Godfrey Rivers Trust, 1936

as a model a young, red-haired, Jewish girl.
Wendy Baron, in her biography of Sickert,
points out that the Little Rachel series was
painted at the same time as the 1907
Mornington Crescent Nudes and the series
have common characteristics in the interior
settings and 'insistent parallelism of their
composition';[3] indeed, Sickert appears
to have tackled each of these subjects on
alternate days.[4] Thus, the Queensland Art
Gallery's *Little Rachel* and the Art Gallery of
South Australia's *Mornington Crescent nude
— contre-jour* are closely related in time. The
Little Rachel series is marked by thick
impasto, forming a mosaic showing the effect
of natural light. *Little Rachel* contrasts in style
with the Queensland Art Gallery's later work
by Sickert, *Whistler's studio, c.* 1925. The painting refers back to Sickert's student days
and the artificial half-light, sense of a moment
in time, and slightly mysterious figures are
reminiscent of his music-hall series of the
1890s.

A 1907 landscape by Spencer Gore was
probably one of a number of his landscapes
influenced by Lucien Pissarro in the summer
of that year.[5] A fine landscape by Lucien
Pissarro, *Tea time, Cold Harbour,* 1916, also
forms part of the collection.

The Gallery has two paintings by Augustus
John, *Village girl* and *Henry John.* The latter is
an appealing portrait of John's son, Henry,
by his first wife, Ida Nettleship. Ida died at
Henry's birth and, alone of John's children,
Henry was brought up outside John's
bohemian circle. The portrait of this intense
and seemingly rather insecure and unhappy
young man was probably painted in the late
1920s or early 1930s, since Henry died by
drowning in 1935.[6]

The British collection contains works
by two Australian-born artists who were
associates of John, a late portrait by Henry
Lamb, and Derwent Lees's *Lyndra in Wales.*
A small flower study by Duncan Grant also
deserves mention. Bernard Meninsky's fine
Cézanne-inspired *Portrait* (Head of a girl) was
painted in the 1940s, a period when the artist
produced some of his most powerful paintings but which ended in his suicide in 1950.
Other interesting British paintings of this
period include Laura Knight's *Mighty lak a
rose,* a portrait study of a black mother and
baby done while on a visit to Baltimore,

above
LUCIEN PISSARRO   TEA TIME, COLD HARBOUR
1916
Oil on canvas   53 × 65cm
Purchased 1959. Annie Chisholm Wilson Bequest

below
STANLEY SPENCER   INTERIOR AT COOKHAM WITH
SPRING FLOWERS
Oil on canvas   51 × 76cm
Purchased 1958. Annie Chisholm Wilson Bequest

HENRY RAEBURN   PORTRAIT OF MAJOR-GENERAL
ALEXANDER MURRAY MACGREGOR AS A YOUNG MAN
c. 1795
Oil on canvas   90 × 68cm
Purchased 1978

and two works by Matthew Smith, a *Fauve*-inspired landscape, and the rhythmic and colourful, *Girl in yellow* (Head and shoulders of a girl), a product of Smith's late and mature style.

Stanley Spencer's *Interior at Cookham with spring flowers* has all the medieval naturalism of detail of his Cookham paintings. Jacob Epstein's *The visitation* is an example of the best of Epstein's religious work, expressing, in his own words, 'a humility so profound as to shame the beholder who comes to my sculpture expecting rhetoric or splendour of gesture'.[7] It is an interesting counterpoint to the primitive power of Epstein's *Woman possessed* in the Australian National Gallery in Canberra.

At present, the Gallery is not strong in later British painting and sculpture, although the Collection has a number of prints and drawings by contemporary British artists including David Hockney, Graham Sutherland, Ben Nicholson, Victor Pasmore and Bridget Riley.

Sculpture includes a small bronze by Henry Moore, a maquette by Barbara Hepworth, representative works by Stuart Brisley and Elizabeth Frink and *Plum line*, a wood assemblage by Nicholas Pope. The Gallery hopes to expand its sculpture collection considerably in the future and to take advantage of the magnificent facilities for large-scale outdoor sculpture provided by the new building.

EDWARD BURNE-JONES   AURORA   1896
Oil on canvas   179 × 76cm
Purchased 1954

[1] This theme was reflected also in early Australian purchases. Josephine Muntz-Adams's *Care* was the first Australian work purchased.

[2] Bruce Laughton, *Philip Wilson Steer 1860-1942*, Oxford, 1971, p. 103.

[3] Wendy Baron *Sickert*, London, 1973, pp. 103-104, 107, 347. The model was probably a Miss Siderman who died in 1963, aged 70. She may have been a frame-maker's daughter.

[4] ibid., p. 103. Baron quotes his letter on this subject to fellow artist Nan Hudson. THe Mornington Crescent nudes, in turn, relate to the Camden Town Murder series.

[5] Baron, *The Camden Town Group*, London, 1978, p. 18.

[6] Malcolm Easton and Michael Holroyd *The Art of Augustus John*, London, 1974, p. 14. The National Gallery of Victoria's portrait of John's daughter *Poppet*, by Dorelia McNeill, is closely related in time.

[7] H. Read (ed.), *Discovering Art: Twentieth Century*, Vol. I, p. 127.

left
JACOB EPSTEIN   THE VISITATION   1926
Bronze   178cm high
Purchased 1958. Miss Estelle Marguerite Cunningham Neilson
Bequest

below
AUGUSTUS JOHN   HENRY JOHN
Oil on canvas   60 × 46cm
Purchased 1953

Jon Molvig: *Self portrait*

by Gordon Shepherdson

This self portrait was painted in 1956 by a man who lived between the years of 1923 and 1970. It is 142 × 114.3 cm, painted on hardboard. The thoughtful, sculptured image breaks from left to right. Painted in warm, sombre, earth colours, it is indeed a very good painting. The placing of the crossed-leg silhouette combined with the exterior landscape is a tribute to Molvig's draughtsmanship, bringing the overall composition of the work to a very high standard indeed.

It would be facetious of me to try to tell what Jon Molvig's intentions were when he painted this work, for the very obvious reason that I am not Jon Molvig. However, I feel that the only way is to tell you what I feel from my own point of view. Self portraits are, in my opinion, vastly different from portraits. It has always been a mystery to me why painters through history continue to produce images of themselves. It could be to please the historians. Maybe I'll find the answer, if I am lucky enough to live a little longer. It has always been hard enough to produce the images and feelings of somebody else, let alone an image of your own soul, for all the world to goggle at.

For me there are only two kinds of paint, good and bad, absolutely nothing in between. It is my opinion this self portrait is an extremely good piece of paint indeed. Portraits, to me, should firstly be good paintings and, if you are lucky enough to crack a likeness or a piece of somebody's soul, this is an added bonus. Jon Molvig's self portrait has a large measure of both. Most self portraits are front-on portraits. Jon Molvig's,

however, is a brooding, seated, crossed-leg silhouette, set in an exterior landscape, which says heaps for his innovative and creative abilities. Any of Jon Molvig's other portraits I have seen have always carried the images beyond the reflection into the soul and paint of the painter. This is also true of this self portrait. In fact, I would venture to say that when he painted it he knew exactly where he was at that time of his stay on the planet. The use of the exterior landscape, the sun and trees, tells me he was indeed plugged straight into his own universe at that particular time. Combine this with a strong silhouette of the soul of the man and you have a very powerful painting. The trick is that, despite all the words, it is a simple self portrait, in a simple landscape, painted with a sure-fire hand! End of chat.

One can never make a good painting bad, or a bad painting good, no matter what one says or writes about it. I am not saying this is the best painting 'Leggoland' has, it is just that it is a painting I enjoy very much, painted by a friend I enjoyed very much. Whatever I have written is not gospel to anybody else but myself, and should be taken as such. In Jon Molvig's history this is one of his earlier works, giving the viewer a short insight into some of the excellent portraits he was to paint in later years. For me, the constant, singular thread in Jon Molvig's work are these very portraits.

JON MOLVIG   SELF PORTRAIT   (1956)
Oil on composition board   142 × 114 cm
Gift of the National Gallery Society of Queensland, 1958

Gordon Shepherdson is a Queensland artist who lives and works in Brisbane.

Australian painting

by Deborah Edwards

For many, the Queensland Art Gallery's Australian painting collection has been rather elusive; naturally, it forms the largest of the Gallery's collections, yet lacked facilities for comprehensive display until 1982.

It is not surprising to find that the growth of this collection has been retarded by Brisbane's isolation from the centres of major artistic activity, by uneven Government funding and by the Gallery's relative lack of wealthy private patronage.

The painting collection now comprises approximately 1,200 works. It contains several unquestionable Australian masterpieces, a body of fine paintings and representative works which form a solid basis for future development.

The collection was founded in 1895 with the gifts of three local artists: Walter Jenner, R. Godfrey Rivers and Oscar Fristrom. The first purchase was made three years later. It was a portrayal of world-weary Motherhood, by Josephine Muntz-Adams, entitled *Care,* a

fitting companion for the Gallery's first British purchase, Blandford Fletcher's conscience-prodding *Evicted*, 1887.

The growth of the collection over the next thirty years reflected its birth: in the first half of its life the Australian painting collection relied heavily upon gifts and the support of a small number of local artists. Acquisitions favoured the conservative art of the day.

Within the context of uneven development, the consistent gifts of ex-Queenslander, Miss M. T. Treweeke, in the 1930s, 1940s and 1950s had a noticeable effect. They included the Gallery's first works by Arthur Streeton, Rupert Bunny and Roland Wakelin. The inclusion of the work of Melbourne painters also helped to redress an imbalance in favour of Sydney representation.

In the 1940s, several other factors combined to give added impetus to this collection. Artistic activity in Brisbane intensified, and the untiring efforts of Daphne Mayo and Vida Lahey to promote the concept of art to a

CONRAD MARTENS   VIEW OF BRISBANE (in 1851)   1862
Watercolour and gouache over pencil on wove paper
32 × 51 cm
Gift of Leonard Darwin, 1913

Deborah Edwards, B.A. (Hons), is Assistant Curator of Australian Art at the Queensland Art Gallery. She is currently researching the work of Queensland artist, Isaac Walter Jenner.

conservative public began to draw some response. The Johnstone and Moreton Galleries opened and the Gallery's first Director arrived.

It is, in fact, only in the last forty years that the acquisition policy for Australian art has become wider ranging and that the finest of the Gallery's Australian paintings have entered the collection.

The Australian colonial collection has benefited from systematic acquisitions since 1970. Perhaps the earliest work in this collection is a serenely attractive watercolour by Conrad Martens, depicting the panorama of *Rushcutters Bay, Sydney, from Darlinghurst*, in 1837. The Gallery is fortunate also in possessing a watercolour by Martens of particular interest to Queenslanders. *A view of Brisbane*, executed twenty-five years later as a gift to Charles Darwin, shows a distant view from the South Brisbane rocks of the struggling town of 2,100 in 1851. The work has been freely adapted from topographically detailed sketches in order to create a painting in harmony with the picturesque ideal, yet this does not impair its historical interest.

The colonial concern to explore pictorially Sydney Harbour, five hundred miles away, is restated in two small oils by Edward Peacock: *The heads of Port Jackson from Vaucluse Bay* and *Sydney from the South Head Road above Rose Bay*, both painted in 1847. Henry Gritten's 1850s view of Hobart, *Early settlement* and H. J. Johnstone's later South Australian subject, *Murray River at Mannum*, 1882, also explore southern landscapes.

The Gallery's representation of colonial portraiture and still life began in a distinguished way with William Dexter's sentimentally forceful *Game*, 1853, and a superior and, as yet, rather mysterious *Portrait of Mary Drysdale*, 1879, by Robert Dowling.

The traditions of nineteenth-century marine painting are highlighted in a late painting by British artist Oswald Brierly and by Walter Jenner's work. *A south sea whale chase*, 1885, is undoubtedly the finest of three works executed by Brierly detailing a hunt which took place at Twofold Bay near Sydney. It depicts the adventure to be had at sea through the romantically conceived struggle of man with nature.

The collection is well endowed with work by Walter Jenner, an artist who was inspired

GEORGE LAMBERT   THE MOTHER   1907
Oil on canvas   205 × 162 cm
Purchased 1965. S. H. Ervin Gift

ERIC WILSON   STOVE THEME   1942
Oil, paper and sand on canvas, collage   97 × 53cm
Gift of the Godfrey Rivers Trust, 1948

by the traditions of German Romanticism and who migrated to Brisbane from England in 1883. The Gallery is currently researching Jenner's work and possesses what is, perhaps, his most significant painting in *Cape Chudleigh, coast of Labrador*, a founding work of the collection of Australian art. In it, Jenner depicts the unearthly frozen regions of the Arctic, relieved only by the tepid warmth of a setting sun.

Representation of nineteenth-century Australian art is most comprehensive with the work of the Heidelberg School of the 1880s and 1890s. Holdings of small land-scapes by Arthur Streeton, Charles Conder, Tom Roberts and Walter Withers are gener-ous and include the unusual *Misty morning,* 1889, by Roberts, *The little jetty,* by Conder, and Streeton's fine *Sunny cove,* 1893. The interest of these painters in their urban environment is glimpsed in a recent acquisition by Withers, *Wet day,* 1894.

In the late 1880s and 1890s a number of Australian artists, including those mentioned above, experimented with the decorative effects of organic *Art Nouveau* motifs and Whistlerian tones. The most sophisticated exponent of this style was Sydney Long, whose *Spirit of the plains* is the Gallery's most important nineteenth-century painting and an Australian masterpiece. Painted in 1897 it is a decorative idyllic work which became one of the most consistently popular of Long's paintings. *Spirit of the plains* reveals a masterly synthesis of certain artistic tendencies of the 1890s: *Art Nouveau*, Symbolist art, and the use of classical mythology.

Long has drawn successfully upon the Australian bush and its wildlife as vehicles for his expression. With its enveloping sense of mystery, slow curve of dancing birds and fluctuating delicate colour, *Spirit of the plains* sounds a particularly melodious note in nineteenth-century Australian painting.

The assumed inadequacy of remaining in Australia propelled a great number of artists overseas in the early decades of the twentieth century, particularly after the creation of the Society of Artists' Travelling Scholarship in 1900, which relieved many artists of the financial strain of studying in Europe.

The most important work by Australian artists in these decades reveals the effects of first-hand experience of the great traditions of European art. The diversity of expatriate activity is well represented in the sonorous *Roc Toul,* 1911, by Impressionist J. P. Russell, *On the beach,* 1909, an academic-Impressionist hybrid, by E. Phillips Fox, and Rupert Bunny's unique *Echo and Narcissus, c.* 1914-19.

Hugh Ramsay's *Portrait of Mrs Robertson* (unfinished), *c.* 1905-06, and George Lam-bert's *The mother* are the Gallery's greatest examples from the work of those artists who returned to Australia. *Portrait of Mrs Robertson* reveals the rich painterly touch, bold brush-strokes and loosening up of technique char-acteristic of Ramsay's finest late paintings, and is, in part, attributable to the influence of Sargent.

George Lambert has created a work of self-conscious mastery in *The mother,* which was on exhibition at the Tate Gallery for many years. Painted in the artist's London studio in 1909, the work depicts Mrs Amy Lambert, sons, Maurice and Constance and colleague, Thea Proctor, and follows the tradition of eighteenth-century group por-traiture in the grand style. It pays tribute to the work of Velasquez and to the Italian Mannerists of the sixteenth century. *The mother* possesses all the Romantic flam-boyance, mastery of line and confidence of Lambert's most significant art.

The Gallery also possesses works which must be numbered amongst the finest of several less prominent artists of the period; for example, Anthony Dattilo Rubbo's *Pea gathering (Kurrajong Heights),* 1913, and *Monday morning,* 1912, by Vida Lahey.

Australia's translation of Renaissance revivalism, which was influenced by Lambert's work, is fixed in *Idle hour,* 1933, an interesting painting executed by Lambert's one-time pupil, Arthur Murch.

Whilst the Queensland Art Gallery possesses characteristic examples of main-stream art of the 1920s and 1930s, holdings of the work of early Sydney modernists and modernists of the 1930s are restricted.

The undoubted strength of the collection lies in its representation of post-war artistic experimentation, particularly in the work of Sydney painters.

Fine examples from Melbourne works of the 1940s are Albert Tucker's almost hallu-cinatory portrayal of squalid life in *Fisher-man's Bend,* 1941, and Arthur Boyd's *Berwick*

IAN FAIRWEATHER   EPIPHANY   1962
Synthetic polymer paint on four sheets of cardboard laid down
on composition board   140 × 203 cm
Purchased 1962

above
PETER PURVES SMITH   NAZIS, NUREMBURG   1938
Oil on canvas   71 × 91 cm
Purchased 1961

right
JOHN OLSEN   JOURNEY INTO THE YOU BEAUT COUNTRY
NO. 2   1961
Oil on composition board   186 × 124 cm
Purchased as H. C. Richards's Memorial Prize
winning entry,   1961

work; the great effectiveness of *Nazis, Nuremburg,* 1938, lies in the irony of its composition. The most meticulous and formal of rituals takes place against a landscape of denuded hills and ruined buildings, and the soldiers' 'Heil Hitler' gestures are echoed in angles of inanimate objects over the surface of the painting.

The Queensland Art Gallery's holdings of William Dobell's work offer excellent insights into the nature of his achievement in portraiture. Paintings held in the Gallery span a forty-year period and include Australia's greatest portrait masterpiece, *The Cypriot,* which was chosen for the Gallery in 1943 by Daphne Mayo, at the artist's studio. The remarkable effectiveness of this work lies in the dialogue between firmly geometric organization of volumes and the nervous tension emanating from the sitter. The heightened intensity of colour and restrained curvilinear grace of *The Cypriot* are superior traits of the work of this period. This restrained masterpiece is joined by *Study of Harold Abbott,* 1929, a solidly modelled, almost semi-heroic portrayal of a painter colleague — part of Dobell's portfolio for the 1929 Society of Artists' Travelling Scholarship Competition —

landscape, 1949. The contribution of the latter work to Australian landscape painting lies in a loving recognition of both the untamed and the comfortably intimate aspects of the Australian environment.

During the 1940s Russell Drysdale was also evolving an intensely personal response to the Australian environment. *Man feeding his dogs,* 1941, is the finest painting Drysdale created during his 'mannerist' period of the 1940s. It is a stark and totally compelling painting in which compositional elements, man and the landscape, have been reduced to bare essentials.

Through completely effective artistic structures *Man feeding his dogs* conveys Drysdale's belief in the tenuous nature of our hold over the Australian outback. This masterpiece is supported by other fine Drysdale paintings: *Back verandah,* 1942, which depicts Australia's laconic outback breed, and *Bushfire,* 1944, in which Australia has become a dead post-drought world.

Echoes of Surrealist art pervade this 1940s response to the landscape. The Surrealist vision also informs an earlier painting by Peter Purves Smith, which is arguably his finest

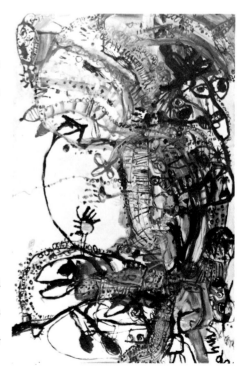

BRIAN DUNLOP   ROOM WITH A VISITOR   1979
Oil on canvas   231 × 327cm
Purchased 1980

and the visually stunning *Portrait of a youth,* *c.*1954. Other works include *Hedley Marston, F.R.S., c.*1952, and *Study in oil for portrait of Dr Norman Behan,* 1970.

Since the commencement of the Archibald Prize in 1921, portraiture has occupied a relatively important, if uninspired, place in Australian art. Two works that greatly advance the Gallery's strong holdings in this area and go far to refute the claim that portraiture is uninspired, are William Dargie's dignified *Portrait of Albert Namatjira,* 1956, loosely handled in vigorous colour, and a contemporary master work by Queenslander Sam Fullbrook, of well-known authoress, *Ernestine Hill,* 1976. The painting is a breathtakingly tender portrayal of both the frailty and directness of this woman.

The Australian collection of the 1940s includes also a significant Douglas Dundas painting, *David Strachan, c.*1946, and a fine group of works by Eric Wilson, highlighting both his representational and abstract concerns. These include the intensely Realist painting, *Still life,* 1934, a competent tribute to teachers Meninsky and Gertler, in *West-minster girl,* 1939; richly impastoed scenes of Paris suburbs, for example, *Snow on the Rue Poulettier,* and, perhaps, a climax in *Stove theme,* 1942. The last-mentioned painting, a result of Wilson's assimilation of the purist theories of Ozenfant, was the first Abstract

painting to enter the Australian painting collection when it was presented in 1948.

Many of those artists who experimented with Abstract principles and dominated the Sydney scene of the 1950s retained, in vary-ing degrees, vestiges of the figurative in their work. Godfrey Miller's formularized *Trees in moonlight,* 1955-58, is a fine example which, in its attempt to echo the perceived unity of light, energy and matter, concentrates on the effects of half-visible and delicate moon-light upon the material world.

John Passmore's Expressionist *Chasing mullet (Air)* and the restrained *Self portrait* by Queenslander Jon Molvig, both painted in 1956, illustrate the disparate concerns of Abstract experimentation of the 1950s. Other very interesting works are *From the gods,* 1955, by Weaver Hawkins and *The raft,* 1956, a brutal, crowded painting by Elwyn Lynn.

Roy de Maistre's *Garden of Gethsemane* could hardly be further removed from the above work. Painted in the 1950s, it is one of the few interesting Australian religious paintings which utilizes an Australian scene. In this case it is Palm Beach, Sydney, painted from memory by the artist in London. It is a cool, stylized painting that demonstrates the essential realism of de Maistre's art.

Ian Fairweather's *Epiphany,* 1962, is effortlessly the finest religous painting in the collection as well as being an Australian

above
SYDNEY LONG   SPIRIT OF THE PLAINS   1897
Oil on canvas on wood   62 × 131 cm
Gift of William Howard Smith in memory of Ormond Charles
Smith, 1940

right
WILLIAM DOBELL   THE CYPRIOT   1940
Oil on canvas   123 × 123 cm
Gift of the Godfrey Rivers Trust, through Miss Daphne Mayo,
1943

below
BRETT WHITELEY   PORTRAIT OF ARTHUR RIMBAUD
1970-71
Oil, gold leaf, synthetic polymer paint, lacquered cat's head and
collage   203 × 518 cm
Purchased 1977

opposite
SAM FULLBROOK   ERNESTINE HILL   1970
Oil on canvas   97 × 76 cm
Gift of the artist, 1972

ARTHUR BOYD   BERWICK LANDSCAPE   1948
Tempera on composition board   70 × 87 cm
Purchased 1977

masterpiece from this period. It is a mature painting, which reveals Fairweather at his most spiritual and complex. *Epiphany* speaks of a deep exploration of Abstract principles. The painting foretells events in the life of the infant Jesus and, if read literally, reveals King Herod, the apprehensive Holy Family and the three bearded Wise Men. Balanced, intricate and restrained in colour, the work creates a world in which all parts are equal and all demand the same intensity of response from the viewer.

The continuing domination of Abstract concerns in Sydney in the early 1960s is summed up in John Olsen's linear Expressionist *Journey into the you beaut country No. 2*, 1961, a richly sensuous and joyful interpretation of the Australian landscape.

The concerns of leading Melbourne painters of the 1960s are pinnacled in Leonard French's rich and deliberate *Autumn in the garden*, 1960-61, and a recently acquired masterpiece by Fred Williams, *Echuca landscape*, 1961, a painting from the early Cubist series, without horizon line and sky area, and consisting of a densely woven forest of vertical sapling shapes.

In recent years, the Queensland Art Gallery

has been extending holdings of modern Australian work in an attempt to come to terms with the diversity of contemporary art practice. Acquisitions have been restricted primarily to paintings and works on paper. The Gallery now possesses a number of fine works that point to the different explorations taking place in the field of Australian painting of the 1970s and 1980s.

Brett Whiteley's self-consciously sensational *Portrait of Arthur Rimbaud*, 1970, is one such example. Modelled on selected images from the romantic child-hero's poetry and utilizing found objects, the painting is, in many ways, a celebration of artistic activity and of Whiteley's own philosophy of the meaning to be found within a partnership of brutal vulgarity and lyrical beauty.

Brian Dunlop's *Room with a visitor* was painted in 1980 when the artist was obviously concerned as much with spaces and the relationship between objects as with the figurative image. It is a contemporary master work in which the eye is effectively pulled over the canvas from one object to another, through relationships of shape and colour.

A haystack, 1982, by Photo-Realist painter William Delafield Cook is a recent major acquisition that minutely details a monumental hay pyramid of complex recesses and projections, framed by its own golden haze.

The Gallery's commitment to contemporary Queensland art is always increasing. One highlight of this collection is *Owl Creek III*, 1979, by Lawrence Daws. This work reveals the strong regional ties felt by many Queensland painters and is the artist's finest lyrical painting to date. Another highlight is the recently acquired painting from the *Anna and dog series* by powerful Queensland painter, Davida Allen.

The Queensland Art Gallery's aim is to provide for its public, insights into the history and traditions of Australian art through the most significant works possible, as well as to encourage a truly personal and worthwhile response to the individual work of art. The Gallery is well aware of the areas of weakness in the collection and the need to correct these deficiencies. While the 1980s have seen an increased commitment to acquiring non-contemporary European paintings, the commitment to consolidating and improving the Australian collection remains unaffected.

Prints, drawings and photography

by Sue Smith

JAMES WHISTLER   FUMETTE   1858
(from *Twelve Etchings from Nature*, The French Set)
Etching, drypoint   16 × 11 cm
Gift of Sir James (Robert) McGregor K.B.E., 1956

Sue Smith is Assistant Curator, Prints and Drawings, at the Queensland Art Gallery.

The Queensland Art Gallery places major emphasis on its prints and drawings collection, which contains approximately 2,000 Australian and international prints, drawings and photographs. The collection was established in the Gallery's early years with a small number of donations, beginning with the Queensland Government's gift, in 1895, of a group of original and reproductive etchings and engravings.[1] Few additions were made in the early decades of the century, until the collection received a fresh impetus in the 1930s with the Queensland Art Fund's gifts of contemporary British and Australian prints and drawings, which were followed by other individual donations (many made through the Fund) in a remarkably public-spirited effort for the Depression years.

The bulk of the collection has been acquired since 1945, with particular emphasis, until quite recently, on Australian and British works. The years from 1978 to 1982 were a major turning point in the history of the development of the collection, as curatorial and conservation staff were appointed (including, from 1979 to 1981, the first Curator of Prints and Drawings, Margaret Lock) and new collecting policies and programmes of documentation, conservation and storage were implemented. The benefits of these policies have been the acquisition of several master works by artists the Gallery might not otherwise represent, such as the lithograph, *Madonna* by Edvard Munch, and the laying of foundations for more extensive collections of works on paper, which will provide, in time, an historical context for viewing more isolated works from other departments in the Gallery.

Prints and Drawings

In 1978, attention was focused on upgrading the European collection, which comprised a small group of works spread thinly over a period of some four hundred years. The holdings included important woodcuts by Dürer, and other Old Master prints by Rosa, Reni, Claude, Ruisdael and Rembrandt; the latter group included works drawn from the 1895 gift and purchases made, on the advice of Dr Ursula Hoff, during the directorship of Laurie Thomas. Later prints included etchings by Goya, Meryon, Millet, Manet and Renoir, lithographs by Daumier, and twentieth-century prints by Kollwitz, Braque, Rouault, Delaunay and Vasarely. Drawings ranged from a group of French and Italian Old Masters purchased in 1954 at the auction of Sir Marcus Clarke's collection to nineteenth- and twentieth-century drawings by Lavezzari, Pascin and Greco.

Preliminary development of this collection was concentrated in the modern period, to provide support for the Gallery's major French paintings and sculpture. From 1978 to 1981, a considerable portion of the total budget for acquisitions was expended on prints dating from about 1850 to 1950. Many outstanding works were acquired, including etchings from Corot to Rouault, and major lithographs of the 1890s.

The modern European print collection contains several works originally issued as illustrations for *de luxe* illustrated books, and it is intended that future acquisitions for the department will include selected *livres d'artistes* to complement important groups of prints and to extend the collection's graphic representation of major artist-printmakers. Other long-term objectives for the European collection include the acquisition of Medieval Illumination and Incunabula and increased representation of Old Master drawings and prints. Recent Old Master purchases include drawings by Boucher, Natoire and van Goyen, which, together with modern European prints and drawings, are discussed in Dr Langer's article.

British and Australian works comprise

above
SAMUEL PALMER   THE BELLMAN
1879
Etching   19 × 25 cm
Purchased 1981

right
JESSIE TRAILL   BEAUTIFUL
VICTIMS   1914
Etching   65 × 49 cm
Purchased 1961

the numerical strengths of the collection, although there are many lacunae which are receiving attention progressively.

Representation is especially sporadic for eighteenth- and nineteenth-century prints, which range from a few works by John Clerk, Hogarth, Barry, Jackson, a group of trial proofs from the *Liber Studiorum* and other sets by Turner, to topographical engravings of exploratory voyages to the Pacific Islands and the eastern coast of Australia. The 'etching revival' in England in the latter part of the nineteenth century is represented by Legros, and by Whistler, with two superb, early etchings: *Fumette*, 1858, and *Rotherhithe*, 1860. Another outstanding etching of the period is Samuel Palmer's *The bellman*, 1879, an exalted dream of village life experienced in youth and recollected in maturity.

The Australian landscape and life on the gold-fields are recorded in lithographs by von Guérard, Ham and Gill; complemented by Gill's drawing of a *Digger's wedding in Melbourne*, which captures the insouciance of a boom period. The existence of the Aborigines is idealized in Duterreau's etching, *A wild native taking a kangaroo*, 1836, and in later drawings by Gill and Martens of Rousseauean idylls. Other drawings of the period include landscape studies by Gill, Martens and Buvelot; a fine portrait of *Eliza Gregory*, attributed to Thomas Bock, *c.* 1845, and exquisitely detailed sheets of a horse, and figure and costume studies by Strutt, probably preparatory sketches for his historical painting, *Black Thursday, 6th February, 1851* in the State Library of Victoria.

British figurative drawings, to the close of the nineteenth century, include early academic studies by Etty and Wright, a graceful sketch of a *Peasant girl with ewer* by Bonington, and two delicate metalpoint drawings of youths by Legros. Landscapes in varying modes — naturalistic, topographical and idealized — are presented in drawings by Wilson, Turner, Gainsborough and Cotman.

Contemporary Anglo-Australian styles of traditionalist etching and relief printing were acquired in the early decades of the twentieth century, many as gifts from an approving public. British etchers represented include Brangwyn, Cameron, Brockhurst, Sickert and John; the Australian movement is represented by Long, Gruner, Ure Smith, Shirlow,

Lionel Lindsay, Norman Lindsay, Dyson and Traill. The resurgence of relief printmaking in the inter-war period is represented by a large group of Australian works, including notable colour prints by Hall Thorpe and Margaret Preston, and a group of wood engravings, mostly of birds, by Lionel Lindsay. The collection includes a few works by British printmakers such as Blair Hughes-Stanton and Agnes Miller-Parker, who exerted an influence on the Australian printmakers.

Western relief printing in the collection is complemented by a group of Japanese Ukiyo-e woodblock prints, depicting a 'floating world' of actors, courtesans and fleeting pleasures. The collection was formed by the close of the 1940s and ranges from a seventeenth-century print by Moronobu to groups by Hokusai, Kunisada and Hiroshige, with a few printed books (including a volume of the *Hokusai Manga*). Ongoing development of the Japanese print collection has been assisted through the gifts and expert advice of many people, including Professor Joyce Ackroyd, Mrs Fuji Chamberlain and Mrs Verlie Just.

With a few exceptions, later Australian printmaking languished until the late 1950s when new directions were found; contemporary printmakers represented with significant numbers of prints include Fred Williams, Earle Backen, George Baldessin, Colin Lanceley and Lloyd Rees. Contemporary British print holdings are not numerous but include several fine works, such as the group of studio proofs of lithographs by Alan Davie, Barbara Hepworth, David Hockney, Allen Jones and others, donated by the Curwen Press in 1979.

Twentieth-century British drawings include a lithe study of a reclining female nude by Jacob Epstein and works by Frank Brangwyn, Lucian Freud, Eric Kennington, William Orpen and Stanley Spencer. Australian drawings from early in the century include works by Arthur Streeton, George Lambert, Hans Heysen and J.J. Hilder; a group of figurative line drawings; an exotic monotype of odalisques, *La danse du voile* by Rupert Bunny; and from the 1930s to the 1950s, drawings by Grace Cossington Smith, Lloyd Rees, Rah Fizelle, William Dobell, Douglas Dundas, Donald Friend, Russell Drysdale and Godfrey Miller, and monotypes by Margaret Preston. A recent trend for spectacularly large drawings is represented

top left
RICHARD PARKES BONINGTON   PEASANT GIRL
WITH EWER
Pencil   25 × 14cm
Purchased 1977

below left
WILLIAM STRUTT   Untitled (Studies of a man and details of costume for *Black Thursday, 6th February, 1851*) c.1861-63
Pencil   26 × 21cm
Purchased 1974

above
THOMAS BOCK (Attrib.)   PORTRAIT OF ELIZA GREGORY
c.1845
Coloured chalks   58 × 42cm
Purchased 1979

above
KUNISADA II   NAKAMURA SHIKAN AS SHUKA   1864
Colour woodcut
Triptych: each panel 36 × 24 cm
Purchased 1976

right
MARGARET PRESTON   HAWKESBURY RANGES, N.S.W.,
WINTER   1946
Colour monotype   35 × 38 cm
Purchased 1948

top left
RUPERT BUNNY   LA DANSE DU VOILE
Colour monotype   24 × 34 cm
Purchased 1982

left
WILLIAM STRUTT   Untitled (Study of a woman's head for
Black Thursday, 6th February, 1851)   c.1861-63
Pencil and watercolour wash   21 × 17 cm
Purchased 1977

above
EDVARD MUNCH   MADONNA   1895-1902
Colour lithograph   55 × 35 cm
Purchased 1981

right
HORST P. HORST   COCO
CHANEL   1937
Gelatin silver photograph
18 × 17 cm
Purchased 1982

below
ROSE SIMMONDS   THE
THREE WITCHES   c. 1930s
Bromoil photograph
31 × 25 cm
Gift of Dr J. H. Simmonds, 1982

with works by George Baldessin, Charles Blackman, William Delafield Cook, John Olsen and Gordon Shepherdson.

The Gallery has been fortunate in acquiring large collections of drawings and other works on paper by Queensland artists, including James Wieneke's studies of Australians at war in the South Pacific for his book, *6th Div. Sketches*[2]; preparatory studies for stained-glass commissions by William Bustard; and drawings and prints by Vincent Sheldon.

Photography

Photographs first entered the collection in 1972, with The Photographic Society of Queensland's gift of a small group of Australian and international prints, which included Yousef Karsh's portraits of Pablo Casals and Georgia O'Keefe. Later collecting was temporarily suspended, pending the Gallery's relocation to the Queensland Cultural Centre, and was resumed in 1982. The brief for the photography collection is wide, within the limitations of funding of the day, and aims to provide a selective representation of major international photographers and photographic movements and a more comprehensive collection of Australian photography, including Queensland photography of aesthetic merit, to complement major historical collections at the John Oxley Library, Queensland Museum, and other institutions. Recent acquisitions include prints by the American portrait and fashion photographer, Horst P. Horst: *Coco Chanel, 1937*, and *Gertrude Stein with Horst, 1946*, contemporary Australian prints by Glen O'Malley and Philip Quirk and prints and transparencies by a Queensland Pictorialist, Rose Simmonds.

The Gallery's display policy is directed towards introducing a wider audience to prints, drawings and photographs in the collection through varied exhibitions held about six times a year. Individual works from the collection may be viewed, by appointment, in the Gallery's study room.

[1] Listed in the *Illustrated Catalogue of the Queensland National Art Gallery*, Brisbane, 1908.
[2] James Wieneke, *6th Div. Sketches: Aitape to Wewak. Being a Collection of Sketches, Drawings and Notes, from the Sixth Australian Division's Last New Guinea Campaign — through Aitape, Maprik and Wewak, 1944-1945*. Written and illustrated by James Wieneke, Sydney, the author, 1946.

Sculpture, crafts and decorative arts in the Australian collection

by Glenn R. Cooke

ROBERT KLIPPEL   METAL SCULPTURE   1972
Mild steel; fabricated by Mr Les Wild, Sydney
218 × 38 × 36 cm
Purchased 1979

Glenn R. Cooke, M.A., is Curator of Decorative Arts at the Queensland Art Gallery. He is currently researching The life and work of L. J. Harvey.

Sculpture

The growth of the Australian sculpture collection of the Queensland Art Gallery, in common with other State collections, has had to take a secondary role to painting. It is interesting, then, to learn that the first major Australian work purchased (in 1912) was Queenslander Harold Parker's lyrical *First breath of Spring.* The nude figure of Spring, which owes something to Rodin in the tenderly realized form contrasting with the roughly chiselled base, awakens from the confines of the wintry marble. Nude figures of young women, clothed only in allegorical or mythological titles, are typical of the covert eroticism of the period but, in Parker's work, we have an inspired synthesis of academic and realist traditions. Though Parker was born in England, he came to Australia at an early age, studied at the Central Technical College, Brisbane and, from 1896, in London. The seal of his success was bestowed by the Chantrey Bequest's acquisition of *Ariadne* for the Tate Gallery in 1908.

A talented fellow student at the Central Technical College was L. J. Harvey. He remained in Brisbane and established a career which lasted for more than fifty years, as a wood carver, sculptor, potter and teacher. A bronze head of his daughter, *Elsie,* possibly his finest work, together with a good example of his pottery, was given by friends and students in 1938. Attention focuses on L. J. Harvey this year in the first major retrospective exhibition to be held at the new Gallery. This exhibition both assesses Harvey's influence and reviews his teaching methods. A number of works by his pottery

students, which demonstrate the range and variety of his techniques, have recently been gifted to the Gallery; these include examples by Mary Lawrence, Alma Williamson, Val McMaster, Frances Dunbar, Ida Martin and Agnes Barker.

With carving techniques such as inlay, piercing and scraffito forming such a major part of the decoration, it is hardly surprising that many of Harvey's students also worked in wood. Daphne Mayo, his foremost student, is represented by ten works, including the classically inspired bronze torso *The Olympian, c.* 1946, and *Portrait of R. Godfrey Rivers.* Daphne Mayo gained considerable fame for her work on the tympanum of the Brisbane City Hall and was instrumental in establishing a travelling scholarship, the beneficiary of which was Leonard Shillam. Both he and his wife Kathleen, Queensland's leading contemporary sculptors, are well represented in the collection by examples of sandstone carving and welded metal work.

The earliest Australian sculptural work in the collection is Bertram MacKennal's fine bronze, *Daphne,* 1897, but, apart from Queensland artists, significant works are not represented until the 1950s. An Epstein-inspired pair of 'Cherubs', *c.* 1956, carved in mountain ash by Ola Cohn, is of special interest. More recent sculptural wood works include Joe Steele's finely crafted and whimsical *Box,* 1976, and the fragile, transient *You Yangs,* 1980, of John Davis. A most important recent acquisition has been Peter Taylor's *Figures in a changing landscape, c.* 1981-82.

Taylor's previous work displayed the

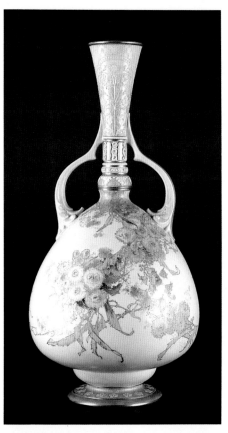

opposite
SONIA DELAUNAY
SYNCOPEE
Cartoon *c.*1964; woven
1973-74
Wool tapestry woven at
Aubusson, France, by Pinton
Felletin   200 × 175 cm
Purchased 1980.
Queensland Art Gallery
Foundation, with funds from the
Queensland Art Gallery Society

right
DOULTON BURSLEM   VASE
*c.*1884-1902
Porcelain decorated with gum
blossoms by Louis Bilton
50 × 23 × 23 cm
Gift before 1935

below
PICKFORD MARRIOTT
LOVE IN HER EYES SITS
PLAYING   1902
Panel in gesso and oil, mother
of pearl and semi-precious
stone   50 × 47 × 8 cm
Purchased 1928

top right
PETER TAYLOR   FIGURES IN A CHANGING LANDSCAPE   *c.*1981-82
Polychromed carved and slab wood in two parts with bronze mask   226 cm high
Purchased 1982 with the assistant of the Visual Arts Board of the Australia Council

above
L. J. HARVEY and his students
Group of pottery
Back row: Frances Dunbar (1928); L. J. Harvey (1928)
Middle row: Ida Martin (1937); Mary Laurence (1925); L. J. Harvey (1927); Val McMaster
(*c.*1935-40)
Front row: Agnes Barker (1933); Agnes Barker (1931); Orma Smith (1933); Alma Williamson (1924)

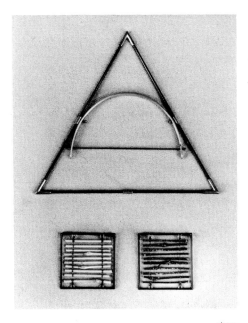

fine grain of Huon pine in formalized manne-quin figures. The mythic imagery of these pieces is retained but the roughly hewn slabs of pine have been covered by splashes of green, yellow, red and blue paint, which both camouflages and abstracts the figures. Contemporary metal sculptures include Lenton Parr's *Rigel*, 1966-67; Inge King's monumental *Great planet*, 1976-77; Guy Boyd's *Swimmer with arms surrounding*; a group of works by Joel Elenberg; Margel Hinder's *Diatropic; Down the chute*, 1978, by Les Kossatz (which was the winning entry in the Andrew and Lilian Pedersen Memorial Prize for sculpture in 1978) and Robert Klippel's important *Metal sculpture*, 1972. The latter work creates the same off-beat elegance as his earliest junk assemblages but is totally fabricated. It is, perhaps, a token of and response to our increasingly mechanistic way of life.

Crafts

Colonial crafts are represented in the collection only by a silver and emu-egg desk-set attributed to Evan Jones and a pair of emu-egg inkwells by C. A. Brown of Brisbane. The latter was recently acquired by the Queensland Art Gallery Foundation and, as the major piece of identified Queensland colonial silver, is a significant addition to the collection.

Crafts in the first half of this century are also meagrely represented. A leather jewel casket by Walter Taylor is an interesting exception.

Contemporary Australian ceramics have been acquired since 1950 and the assistance of the Queensland Art Gallery Society in this area is especially appreciated. John Perceval's *Herald angel*, Arthur Boyd's tile *The baptism*, a red stoneware vase by Shigeo Shiga and a fine group of works by David and Hermia Boyd deserve special mention. This last group

demonstrates consummate craftsmanship in the finely thrown shapes and a refined sensibility of decoration with simple glazes, vigorous brushwork or delicate scraffito designs. The acquisition of works by local potters has been a continuing interest. Carl McConnell, Warren Palmer, Errol Barnes, Lyndal Moore and Bruce Anderson, among others, are represented by fine and typical works.

The Queensland Art Gallery expressed its interest in Australian craft by sponsoring a major Survey of Contemporary Australian Craft for the period of the Commonwealth Games. This involved selecting one hundred and seventy-five items from the areas of ceramic, textile/fibre and metalwork/jewellery.

The ceramic complement of the Survey amplifies the scope of the works already in the collection and contains such fine works as

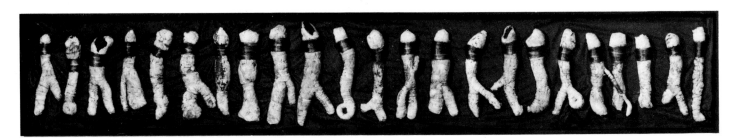

Alan Peascod's *Form,* Sandra Taylor's *Bella casa*, Alan Watt's *Cloud Series I & II* and Phillip McConnell's *Blossom jar.*

The textile category contains what is possibly the best work in the Crafts Survey: Jutta Feddersen's *Mumien 24.* The bound forms of fibre and human hair in this work have a unique and disquieting power. Barbara Macey's quilt, *Wave 7,* Margaret Ainscow's *Kimono I* and Kay Lawrence's tapestry in five panels, *A walk around the inside looking out* (which was recently exhibited in the 'Lodz Textile Triennale' in Poland) are other highlights.

The metal-work/jewellery complement contains Matcham Skipper's *Chalice and paten,* Peter Tully's *Masi moments III,* Carlier Makigawa's refined *Articulated bracelet and brooches,* Susan Cohn's *Armrings* and Norman Creighton's *Strathavon game.* The textile and metal-work components will form the nucleus for further contemporary acquisitions.

Glass promises to be one of the most exciting areas of craft development in the near future, and a gift of $20,000 by Australian Consolidated Industries makes it possible for the Gallery to acquire works by contemporary glass artists. Julio Santos, Stan Melis, Warren Langley and Giselle Courtney are among those already represented.

Decorative Arts

As the Queensland Art Gallery has had to depend on gifts and bequests as the basis of its small decorative arts collection, it is to be expected that representation is erratic. It was not until Robert Haines became Director in 1952 that decorative arts were actively purchased.

The collection of silver and Sheffield plate bequeathed by Colonel F. D. Le M. Gostling in 1942 provides a representative coverage of the Georgian and Victorian periods. A pair of repoussé stirrup cups presented to an ancestor in 1861 is the finest item in the bequest. A Scottish bullet-shaped tea-pot by J. MacKay (dated 1781-82), a coffee-pot by Fuller White (dated 1755-56), a presentation urn by William Elliott (dated 1814), and the recent purchase of a tea-caddy by Pierre Gillois, 1772, have added greater interest to the collection.

More than forty items of furniture were bequeathed by Mrs Blanche Buttner in 1972

HAROLD PARKER   FIRST BREATH OF SPRING   1911
Marble   62 × 48 × 25 cm (with base)
Purchased 1912

above
STAN MELIS   SEA FORM   1982
Hot blown and worked glass   12 × 22 × 19 cm
Purchased 1982. Queensland Art Gallery Foundation with funds
donated by A.C.I. Glass Pty Ltd

right
SONY MANNING   VASE   1982
Porcelain, slipcast inlaid and fired in oxidized atmosphere to
1220° centigrade   28 × 9 cm diameter
Purchased 1982 with the assistance of the Crafts Board
of the Australia Council

to form the core of the furniture collection. This group spans the period from the seventeenth to the nineteenth centuries and includes a William IV mahogany card-table and continental marquetry chest of drawers. The Queensland Art Gallery intends to acquire several very fine items of furniture, which will become the focus of the existing collection.

Forty-three items of Bohemian glass were bequeathed by Dr Ernest Singer in 1975 and provide the greatest interest in the glass collection, with their variety of coloured bodies and fine quality engraving. Other items of note include a superb Waterford-style table stand, an Arts and Crafts period glass with green, trailed decoration, and a Venetian or Austrian enamelled tall vase recently gifted by Mrs L. Taylor.

Sir Henry Doulton gave twenty-seven items of his factory's production to the Queensland Government in 1892. These were transferred to the newly established Gallery in 1895 and, together with the gift of two terracotta biblical panels by George Tinworth and a Chang vase by John Shorter in 1933, provide the strongest group in the ceramic collection.

Dr Singer's bequest also provided a range of lace and embroidery items which improved the existing collection. The most significant item in the textile collection, however, is the dynamic tapestry, *Syncopée,* by Sonia Delaunay given by the Queensland Art Gallery Society in 1980. Delaunay became known as one of the most brilliant designer-decorators of this century and, together with her husband, Robert, was responsible for the movement known as 'Orphism'. *Syncopée* is a typical work in its syncopated rhythm of concentric, contrasting and harmonizing colours. It is intended that the textile collection will develop as a resource for Queensland textile artists and students.

Other gifts and purchases over the years have added important items to these collections, especially in 1968 when a group of contemporary works was acquired from the 'Design in Scandinavia' exhibition.

Considering the range of items already represented in the collection, it is envisaged that decorative arts will focus on the traditions of Europe and Australia but include fine examples from other cultures.